SUNDAY.

THE NEW TESTAMENT MADE EASY

A 60-DAY BIBLE STUDY TO GROW YOUR FAITH

ZACH WINDAHL

BETHANY HOUSE
a division of Baker Publishing Group
www.BethanyHouse.com

Published by Bethany House Publishers
Minneapolis, Minnesota
BethanyHouse.com

Bethany House Publishers is a division of
Baker Publishing Group, Grand Rapids, Michigan

Printed in the United States of America

ISBN 978-0-7642-4243-4 (paper)

Library of Congress Cataloging-in-Publication Control Number: 2023030987

This book contains original material as well as excerpts from *The Bible Study: Part Two: New Testament* by Zach Windahl, published by The Brand Sunday, 2017; *Sunday School: The Basics* by Zach Windahl, published by The Brand Sunday, 2020; and *The Bible Study: Youth Edition* by Zach Windahl, published by The Brand Sunday, 2019.

Cover design by Katlyn Hovland

Baker Publishing Group publications use paper produced from sustainable forestry practices and post-consumer waste whenever possible.

24 25 26 27 28 29 30   7 6 5 4 3 2 1

CONTENTS

Introduction

I know that God aligned our paths on purpose, and I couldn't be more excited about what He is going to do in your life during this sixty-day journey together through the New Testament.

My prayer is not only for you to have a better understanding of the Word, but also that you will find a better sense of meaning for your life and really understand the heart of our Father. He loves you so much and is delighted that you want to spend time getting to know Him through Scripture.

The focus of this study is to hold your hand as you read the New Testament from Matthew through Revelation. All you need is a Bible and this workbook. The content is intended for anyone who wants to understand the New Testament better. No matter your age or the depth of your relationship with Jesus, I believe you will learn something new in these sixty days.

Before fully diving into the books of the New Testament, we will begin by looking at the basics of Christianity, the big-picture story of the entire Bible, and an overview of the New Testament.

Every day you will be assigned to read three to six chapters from the Bible, depending on their size. Don't worry, I spaced them out so that the reading is manageable. Once you have read the text, you will spend fifteen to thirty minutes journaling your responses to the questions for the day. At the end of each week, there will be a recap to see how you are feeling.

One final note: Just like you, I want to know the truth, so I spend a lot of my time soaking in the Word of God and researching views of scholarly believers around the world. I love studying, really. It brings me to life. With that said, this study is a compilation of material I have gathered over the last few years and translated into modern terms to help better your understanding (and mine) of the text. While many of the details are not agreed upon by all scholars and Bible students, such as the dates of writing of a particular book or even the details of an author, what I have included here is a reflection of my intensive study. By no means am I an expert or a scholar. I just love helping people further their faith in Jesus Christ, our Lord and Savior.

That's it! That's all I've got for you. Enjoy!
Zach

Basics of Christianity

Before we get started, we need to build the foundation of our faith. The following seven pillars are the starting point for understanding the Bible and growing in your relationship with God, whether you recently accepted Jesus as your Savior or have been practicing Christianity your entire life.

God the Father ☀ and what it means to be a child of God.

Jesus Christ ✝ and how He saved you and me.

The Holy Spirit 🔥 and the power we are given.

The Bible 📖 and the story of humanity as a whole.

Prayer 🙏 and how we communicate with God.

Grace 💕 and the favor that is placed upon us.

Community 👥 and the importance of doing life with others.

GOD THE FATHER

Also known as Lord God, YHWH, Abba, Elohim, Jehovah, Ancient of Days, Most High, El-Shaddai, Adonai

Who Is God the Father?

First things first. To understand who God is, you need to understand that He consists of three equal persons: God the Father, God the Son, and God the Holy Spirit. This is called the *Trinity*. There is nothing in our reality that we can compare it to, which makes understanding the three-part nature of God fairly difficult. Many theologians have tried to break it down into analogies, such as water, ice, and mist, or all the pieces of an egg: shell, yolk, and egg white. All of which have their own purpose separately as well as their purpose together. Our God, the one true God, is Three in One.

The initial person of the Trinity is God the Father. We see God the Father predominantly in the first section of the Bible, called the Old Testament, where we begin to understand the nature of God. We see him as holy, faithful, just, and all-knowing, and as a protector, friend, provider; He is a true father figure to His children, pouring out unconditional love on them.

What Does That Mean for Me?

God the Father loves His Son, Jesus, more than anything in the world. Since we have accepted Jesus into our lives and we are now viewed through the lens of Jesus (which we will look at next), God the Father loves us in exactly the same way, as one of His own children. So we are called "children of God" (1 John 3:1). This is the best news ever. No matter what your relationship with your earthly father is, God calls you His child and wants to love you even better.

Not only is God now our eternal Father figure, but all sorts of blessings come along with that. We are loved, provided for, and protected. Scripture says that we are co-heirs (Romans 8:17), new creations (2 Corinthians 5:17), and holy priests (1 Peter 2:5). There is nothing we can do to run away from the love of the Father. It's eternal and unconditional. All we have to do is accept it.

JESUS CHRIST

Also known as Christ, Savior, Messiah, Son of God, Son of Man, Emmanuel, the Word, Redeemer

Who Is Jesus Christ?

The second person of the trinity is God the Son, Jesus Christ. To understand the importance of Jesus, you need to have a big-picture understanding of the whole story.

In the beginning, God created two people: Adam and Eve. He placed them in an area called the Garden of Eden, which they were to cultivate. In the Garden, Adam and Eve had a perfect relationship with God. One day a serpent came on the scene and convinced them to go against God's plan (God always gives us the choice to obey His Word or not to). . . . Adam and Eve sinned. In Christianity, this event is called the *fall of man*, and that one decision changed the course of humanity because it put a barrier between man and God. As a response, God said that one day He would provide a Son through Eve who would crush the serpent's head and the serpent would bite his heel. This may be confusing but stick with me.

Fast-forward in the first book of the Bible, Genesis, we meet a gentleman named Abraham. God said that through Abraham was going to be the birth of a new nation, God's chosen people. One of Abraham's sons was named Judah, and God promised that the Savior would come through the line of Judah. A while later, God explains things even more and says that the Savior will be from the line of King David. At this time in history, God's presence resided in the temple (for the most part) and very few people could have a personal relationship with God, as Adam and Eve did before the Fall of Man.

In the second section of the Bible, called the New Testament, we are introduced to a man named Jesus. This is the Messiah, the Savior, the Chosen One whom the people have been waiting for since the Fall. Jesus was there to redeem humanity. He was 100 percent man and 100 percent God.

Jesus was born of a virgin, lived a sinless life, and was crucified for the sins of mankind. The shedding of His sinless blood was necessary to pay for all of our sins. So now, if we have accepted Jesus into our heart, when

God the Father looks at you and me, He sees His Son, Jesus, spotless and redeemed. Jesus rose from the dead on the third day and ascended to the right hand of the Father in heaven, and will one day return again for His "bride," the church, and will restore earth to its original intent forever.

What Does That Mean for Me?

This is incredible news for us because by believing in Jesus alone and turning from our sins, we are saved from God's wrath and given eternal life. We don't have to perform for God to bless us. He just loves us as we are.

THE HOLY SPIRIT

Also known as Holy Ghost, Helper, Comforter, Intercessor, Spirit of God, Spirit of Truth, Dove, Presence of God

Who Is the Holy Spirit?

The third person of the Trinity is the Holy Spirit, God's presence and power on earth today. We first see the Holy Spirit hovering over the chaos at the beginning of the Bible before anything or anyone was created. Then we begin to see the Spirit come upon different people throughout the Old Testament, enabling them to do great and wondrous things. In the New Testament, when Jesus was baptized, the Holy Spirit descended from heaven and rested upon Him in the form of a dove. The Spirit remained with Jesus for the rest of His life, which allowed Him to produce good fruit and perform miracles, such as healing the sick, prophesying, and raising people from the dead.

When Jesus left the earth, the Spirit descended upon all his disciples, empowering them to also perform miracles and lead others to Jesus. The Spirit is still present today, alive and active, moving in ways that our minds can't even comprehend.

What Does That Mean for Me?

Just as the Holy Spirit descended upon the disciples back then, He descends upon those of us who believe today and empowers us to do things we can't do on our own. He is our Helper, Teacher, Guide to truth, and He encourages us to share our faith. He gives us spiritual gifts, produces godly characteristics within, and even uses us in supernatural ways to share God's love with others. The more time you spend in God's presence, the more He will use you in incredible ways.

THE BIBLE

Also known as the Word, Word of God, Holy Book, Scripture, Canon, Sword, the Good Book

What Is the Bible?

To put it simply, the Bible is God's Word. It tells the story of God's love for humanity. The Bible is accurate, authoritative, inspired by the Holy Spirit, and applicable to our everyday lives.

The layout of the Bible is a collection of sixty-six books, split into two sections called the Old Testament and the New Testament. The Old Testament contains thirty-nine books that tell the history of God's chosen people, Israel, and the struggles they went through when choosing to do life with and without God's help. The New Testament contains twenty-seven books that describe the life of Jesus and the early church. Even though there are two major sections of the Bible, the overarching theme of the story is God's desire for humanity to know Him, love Him, and trust Him. The Bible ends by telling us about a day in the future when Jesus will return and restore everything.

Why Should I Study the Bible?

The Bible is the most important book you could ever read and study. The more time you spend in it, the more God will speak to you through His Word. Its purpose is to teach you, correct you, and develop you into the person God made you to be. It answers questions, brings clarity, teaches us about God, and shows us that He has a plan for us. The key will be to not get overwhelmed by such a big book. It might not all make sense at first, but keep diving in and your life will be changed for the better.

PRAYER

Also known as Intercession, Invocation, Devotion, Communication, Conversation, Direct Access

What Is Prayer?

Prayer is conversation with God. To put it as simply as possible, prayer is when you talk to God. And you can tell Him everything. He isn't afraid of your thoughts or your situation. Since He is all-knowing, nothing will shock Him. Nothing is too big or too small to pray about because God wants to be involved in every part of your life. You can ask for help, guidance, clarity, forgiveness, wisdom, or just share about how grateful you are. Prayer doesn't have to be long and drawn out. It can be short and sweet if you'd like it to be. All God wants is for you to talk to Him with an open heart and be transparent with your thoughts and feelings.

Why Should I Pray?

Not only is the ability to pray a miracle in itself because you are able to talk directly to the God of the universe, but prayer also changes your life in many other ways too.

Prayer gives us strength.
Prayer leads to breakthroughs.
Prayer makes us more like Jesus.
It builds our relationship with God.
It provides restoration.
It brings forgiveness.
God speaks back to us when we speak to Him.

 **GRACE**

Also known as Favor, Acceptance, Purpose, Kindness, Blessing, Compassion, Mercy

What Is Grace?

Grace is the unmerited favor of God upon our lives. It's what saves us. There is nothing we can do to earn God's grace. It's a free gift from Him.

Why Is Grace Important?

To understand God's grace, think back to before you accepted Jesus into your heart. As a sinner, guilty of breaking God's laws and deserving of death, the only way to redeem your soul was through Jesus.

Enter *grace*.

When we trust in Jesus to save us, God by His grace forgives us of our sins and transforms us into new creations completely—the old is gone, the new has come. And although we still sin and make mistakes, grace also equips us to walk out the plans God has for our lives. We don't deserve grace, but God gives it to us anyway because He loves us unconditionally.

# COMMUNITY

Also known as Body, Church, Gathering of Saints, Bride of Christ, Assembling of Believers

What Is Community?

Christian community is special. There's nothing like it when it's done well. Christian community refers to a group of people who have been united through faith in Jesus. It's the church, whether big or small. Community functions to support people in their faith journey and to grow together. It's a safe place for people to be taught, encouraged, and corrected in their faith.

Why Should I Be Part of a Church Community?

Every Christian should be part of a church community because the Christian faith was not meant to be lived alone. Life is meant to be done with others. And getting plugged into a solid Christian community will only push you further along in your relationship with God. A healthy community will help you when you are down, build you up, be a shoulder to cry on, celebrate alongside you, and answer your questions about God.

Once you pick a church community in your area that you want to be a part of, there are multiple ways you can get involved. You can serve on a team, attend a small group, take a next-steps class, or just begin by having meals with other people in the community. If you don't know where to start, ask a church staff member and they can help point you in the right direction.

Big-Picture Story of the Bible

One of the most important things you can do for your faith is have a big-picture understanding of the Bible as a whole. Then, as you're diving deeper, you'll have a big-picture understanding of each book to always bring it back to the full story that's taking place: the story of God's love for his people.

In one sentence, the main theme of Scripture is that God created something beautiful, humanity chose to go against His plan, and the rest of the story is about God chasing after His people, of which we see a full restoration at the end.

Paradise → disobedience → restoration → paradise again

To start things off, in the beginning of the Bible we see that there is chaos all over the earth, and out of that chaos God begins to create order through light and land and life. He creates an area called the Garden of Eden, which is a place of perfection. He was present, and everything inside the Garden was performing as originally intended. God created a man named Adam and a woman named Eve. They were ordered to create a family and cultivate the Garden. They were to fill the earth and live in perfect relationship with God.

But one day a serpent came on the scene and convinced them to go against God's plan. God always gives us a choice—to obey His Word or not to. To choose good or evil. And Adam and Eve chose evil. They sinned.

In Christianity, this event is called the *Fall of Man*, and that single decision changed the course of humanity because it put a barrier between man and God. As a response, God said that one day He would create a Son through Eve who would redeem all of humanity in the eyes of God.

Fast-forward in the story and we meet a man named Abraham. God said that through Abraham he was going to birth a new nation, God's chosen people, covered in God's blessings. And it was through his family that God was going to bring restoration to the world. The family grows and grows, and the people end up in slavery in Egypt. God uses a man named Moses to set them free from slavery through a series of miracles.

The people wander through the desert for a while, and God gives them what is called the Law. It's basically a rulebook on how to live a holy life that is pleasing to God. By following the Law, the Israelites stood out among their neighbors and represented a new, countercultural way to live.

We see God's people, the Israelites, arrive at an area called the Promised Land, "a land flowing with milk and honey" (Joshua 5:6). It was supposed to be amazing, but the people continued to disobey God and chose evil instead.

In the rest of the Old Testament, which is the first section of the Bible, we see the story line going up and down and up and down. The people chose good and then evil, then good, then evil. It's a pattern that reflects their wanting to do things on their own instead of following what they have been told is right.

The Israelites end up in exile again, this time under the new world power called Babylon. We're then introduced to a bunch of prophets who speak to the people on behalf of God, saying that if they turn from evil He will deliver them through a Messiah, a Savior. But that person didn't show up right away. It was quite a while before He did, actually. God went silent for four hundred years. It's not that He wasn't moving, He just wasn't speaking to His people.

In the first four books of the New Testament, the Gospels, we meet Jesus, and He teaches us how to bring the kingdom of God into our everyday life.

The authorities didn't like Jesus, though, and didn't believe He was truly the Son of God, so they killed Him. But little did they know that the shedding of His sinless blood was necessary because on the cross He bore the sins of all of humanity to cancel out our debt. So now, if we accept Jesus into our heart, when God the Father looks at you and me, He sees His Son, Jesus, spotless and redeemed.

Jesus then rose from the dead on the third day. This is the most significant moment in all of history, and our lives will never be the same because of it. Jesus defeated the power of sin and death, saving us, and allowing us to have a future alongside Him. Because of this, we become new creations spiritually.

The Bible's story ends with full restoration of the earth itself; all the evil we allowed to consume it will be destroyed.

So that's the big-picture story of the Bible. Once you know that, you are able to see how each story throughout the Bible plays into the big picture and, ultimately, what part you have to play in it all.

New Testament Overview

- 27 Books
- Greek language
- First century AD

Gospels

Matthew

Mark

Luke

John

Acts

Acts

Pauline Epistles

Romans

1 Corinthians

2 Corinthians

Galatians

Ephesians

Philippians

Colossians

1 Thessalonians

2 Thessalonians

1 Timothy

2 Timothy

Titus

Philemon

Hebrew Christian Epistles

Hebrews

James

1 Peter

2 Peter

1 John

2 John

3 John

Jude

Revelation

Revelation

Key Figures in the New Testament

JESUS CHRIST

Jesus Christ is the Messiah, God in the flesh. His ministry spanned over three years, but the impact of it is timeless. Jesus came to earth to redeem humanity back into a right relationship with God. You will learn more about Him in the first four books we will study together, the Gospel accounts of Matthew, Mark, Luke, and John.

DISCIPLES

The word *disciple* means "a follower or student of a teacher, leader, or philosopher," according to a quick Google search (English dictionary provided by Oxford Languages). When we talk about the disciples of Jesus, we refer to His twelve closest friends while on earth. They were Andrew, Bartholomew, James son of Zebedee, James son of Alphaeus, John, Judas Iscariot, Jude the brother of James, Matthew, Peter, Philip, Simon the Zealot, and Thomas. One thing to note is that the disciples were quite young, likely between the ages of thirteen and thirty.

JOHN THE BAPTIST

John the Baptist was a prophet who arose after the four hundred years of silence that followed the words of Malachi. He was the forerunner of Christ who was to pave the way and prepare the people for Jesus's arrival. John the Baptist was also Jesus's cousin.

JOHN

John was known as the *beloved disciple* because of how much Jesus loved him. He was faithful until the end and was entrusted with taking care of Mary, the mother of Jesus. He wrote one of the Gospels, three letters to churches in Asia Minor, and the book of Revelation.

PAUL

Paul was known as the Hebrew of Hebrews, having studied under Gamaliel, a revered rabbi and member of the Sanhedrin, and was an extreme Pharisee, which meant he took his religion very seriously. Paul experienced a radical conversion to Christ (which we will read about in the book of Acts), and he became the greatest missionary of the early church. Paul founded many churches around the Greco-Roman world, and today we have letters to some of those churches that give us the groundwork for our theology.

LUKE

Luke was a physician as well as a friend and travel associate of Paul's during a portion of his missionary work. Luke was a Gentile (non-Jewish person), according to many scholars, which would make him the only Gentile author in the New Testament, writing a Gospel account and the book of Acts. Some scholars believe he wrote both letters as testimonies for Paul's Roman trial.

PETER

Peter was one of the first disciples Jesus called to follow Him. Jesus knew that Simon would be a great voice for the kingdom. So He changed Simon's name (meaning *reed*) to Peter (which means *rock*), and although Peter had his ups and downs, he gave us some amazing words recorded in his sermon on the day of Pentecost (which we will read in Acts) and in his two follow-up letters, 1 Peter and 2 Peter.

TIMOTHY

Timothy was Paul's spiritual son and was greatly loved by Paul. Timothy also helped write several of Paul's letters and had two letters written to him by Paul as encouragement to stand strong in the faith and continue with the gospel message.

JAMES

James was a brother of Jesus who didn't believe Jesus was the Messiah until after His resurrection. James then became one of the top leaders for the church in Jerusalem and was highly respected among other believers. He ended up writing the book of James as wisdom literature to be added to the New Testament. It has been said that after he was martyred, his friends saw his knees for the first time, and they were like the knees of a camel from spending so much time in prayer.

60-DAY GOALS

Regardless of what you have done in the past, what matters is *now*. God loves you so much and is so delighted that you want to spend time getting to know Him through Scripture.

▶ Where are you currently in your faith journey?

▶ When you think of the Bible, what comes to mind?

▶ List three things you want to get out of this study.

    1.

    2.

    3.

Gospel of Matthew

AUTHOR

The author of the first Gospel in the New Testament was Matthew, a disciple and former tax collector.

DATE

Matthew wrote his Gospel around AD 50 to 55, most likely from Antioch, according to some scholars.

AUDIENCE

The content of Matthew is heavily focused on Jesus being the Messiah, the King of the Jews, indicating that his audience was likely almost completely Jewish.

REASON

Matthew was written to show the Jewish people that Jesus was the Messiah they had been waiting for.

THEME

Jesus is the Jewish Messiah, the fulfillment of Old Testament prophecy.

KEY VERSE

"Do not think that I have come to abolish the Law or the Prophets; I have not come to abolish them but to fulfill them" (Matthew 5:17).

The Gospel of Matthew is the first book in the New Testament, which is important because Matthew is a Jewish man writing to a Jewish audience, and he shows them that their Messiah has arrived. In Judaism, they believed that one day God would send a person to bring God's kingdom to earth in an act of complete redemption. This person was known as the Messiah, and God's people had been prophesying about His arrival for thousands of years, expecting Him to arrive with force, taking over the government. But as you'll see toward the end of the Gospel, Jesus came in a different way.

The Gospel of Matthew is a phenomenal book of fulfillment. One thing to remember when looking at the four Gospels is to put yourself in the shoes of the original readers so you can better understand what is being taught. In this case, Matthew uses far more Old Testament quotes than the other Gospel writers and doesn't feel obligated to explain the Jewish lifestyle. The audience would have understood all of what he said. If you're newer to the Bible, the Gospel of Matthew will mention a few things that may not make sense right now but will be learned at a later time.

Toward the end of the book, the last words of Jesus that Matthew records are "All authority in heaven and on earth has been given to me. Go therefore and make disciples of all nations, baptizing them in the name of the Father and of the Son and of the Holy Spirit, teaching them to observe all that I have commanded you. And behold, I am with you always, to the end of the age" (28:18–20).

This statement is what is known as the Great Commission. And it's what we've been charged with as well: to make disciples, to baptize them, and to teach them about the Bible. It's our calling, to keep it all about Jesus.

The Gospel of Matthew is all about Jesus. As a Jew. For the Jews. The climax of faith. Matthew is a genius in his writing because he displays one prophecy after the next from the Old Testament, confirming that Jesus Christ is the one true Messiah they had all been waiting for. From the location of His birth to His means of transportation into Jerusalem as the King—it *is* all there and it *has been* all there. From the beginning, God promised a Messiah would come one day and save His people. Jesus is the One. The sad fact is that many people missed it. They couldn't comprehend that the Messiah had actually come because He didn't present himself as a conquering king and do what everyone expected.

As we see time and time again, Yahweh is a God of second chances. He knows it's hard for us to accept things, especially something as brilliant as the advent of the Messiah, the first time around. The good news is that He is coming back. He will come one day to reign supreme and judge every person accordingly.

But until then, keep studying this book! ■

DAY 1

Read Matthew 1–4

▶ Why do you think Matthew began with the genealogy of Jesus?

▶ Have you been baptized? If not, does the story of Jesus's baptism inspire you to one day be baptized?

▶ Satan tried to tempt Jesus with three things. How did Jesus respond each time?

    1.

    2.

    3.

▶ Jesus said "follow me" to Simon (Peter) and Andrew, and they left everything behind to follow Him. What was it about Jesus that made them do such a thing?

▶ Which verse from the Beatitudes (Matthew 5:1–12) stood out to you most? Explain.

▶ When you meditate on the phrase *kingdom of heaven*, what comes to mind?

▶ Jesus spoke of living a life focused on producing "good fruit." Would you say your life currently produces good fruit? If not, what can be improved?

▶ Jesus spoke and people were healed; He spoke and the storm was calmed; He spoke and demons left people. As you are reading this, perhaps for the first time, what is running through your mind?

DAY 3

▶ What is a disciple?

▶ List the twelve disciples below.

1. _____   7. _____

2. _____   8. _____

3. _____   9. _____

4. _____   10. _____

5. _____   11. _____

6. _____   12. _____

▶ Do you take a day for rest every week (a Sabbath)? Why or why not?

▶ Have you ever witnessed a miracle? What happened?

▶ Why do you think Jesus spoke in parables? (Matthew 13:13–17)

▶ Jesus compared the kingdom of God to many different things (see chapter 13). Which example made the most sense to you?

▶ There have been many miraculous stories mentioned in your reading so far. Which one do you find most interesting? Why?

▶ Jesus fed five thousand men and then four thousand men with only a few items. What did He begin with? How much was left over? Do you think there is significance in those numbers?

DAY 5

▶ Why did Jesus call Peter "Satan"? Does that seem harsh?

▶ Matthew describes the Mount of Transfiguration experience, including the appearance of Elijah and Moses talking with Jesus. What do you think our glorified bodies will be like? Will our appearance be different? How old do you think we will be?

▶ If you were the rich young man, would you struggle with what Jesus told you?

▶ Did anything surprise you about Jesus's actions in today's reading?

▶ Why do you think Jesus rode into Jerusalem on a donkey?

▶ What did Jesus do when He entered the temple? Why?

▶ How did Jesus describe His second coming (Matthew 24:29–31)?

▶ Do you think Jesus will return during your lifetime?

DAY 7

▶ What did you learn from the parable of the talents (Matthew 25:14–30)?

▶ Who betrayed Jesus? Why do you think he did it?

▶ Do you think Pilate believed Jesus was the Messiah?

▶ In what ways are you fulfilling the Great Commission (Matthew 28:16–20)? How can you improve?

WEEKLY CHECK-IN & PRAYER

▶ What is the most important thing you learned this past week?

▶ How can you apply the teaching to your life?

▶ Write a short prayer for the week ahead.

Gospel of Mark

AUTHOR

The Gospel of Mark was written by Mark, also known as John Mark. Mark assisted on missionary journeys, and after an early desertion, he was later referred to by Paul as one of his "fellow workers" (Philemon 24) and described as "very useful" to him for ministry (2 Timothy 4:11).

DATE

There is a lot of debate about which Gospel was written first. Some believe that Matthew and Luke were first, with Mark pulling his stories from them. Others believe that Mark wrote first, and Matthew and Luke drew from his account. We do not know for sure the Gospel writing order, but Mark's Gospel was likely written between AD 55 and 59.

AUDIENCE

This Gospel was written to Christians in Rome. If Mark was written at a later date, we know that there were thousands of Christians being martyred in Rome at the time. We also know that the early church met down in the catacombs, the graveyard of martyrs—a stark reminder of the risk they were taking. Mark might have read this Gospel to the other believers there. Think about how much more impactful that would make the story.

REASON

Mark shows Jesus as a suffering Servant to encourage the readers to press on through any form of persecution they were dealing with. He shows the power and actions of Jesus more than the other Gospels to prove this Servant was truly the King.

THEME

Jesus as the suffering Servant.

KEY VERSE

"For even the Son of Man did not come to be served but to serve, and to give his life as a ransom for many" (Mark 10:45).

OVERVIEW

Mark is a unique book in that it highlights miracles far more than teachings. He includes at least eighteen miracles in these sixteen chapters, with only four to ten parables (tallies vary depending on who is counting and how) and one major discourse. Mark does not give any of Christ's ancestry, since the theme is that Christ is a servant, and people didn't care about a servant's ancestry. None of the Gospels identify the author because they don't want the attention to be on themselves. Mark is in this same category.

So, who was Mark?

Mark was too young to be a disciple, but he was fascinated with Jesus, so he hung around Him as much as possible.

You could say that Mark was hyperactive. The word *immediately* is repeated forty-one times—Mark was always on the go from one place to the next. He couldn't sit still, and wanted to be front and center in all of the action, and maybe that's why the book of Mark focuses so heavily on the actions of Jesus instead of on His sermons.

Toward the end of the Gospel, Mark narrows his focus and really displays the reason for Christ's arrival in Jerusalem. Mark gives us the most in-depth look at the final week of Jesus's ministry found in the Gospels. Jesus knew what was going to happen, and it wasn't going to be pretty. His life was to be laid down as an exchange for all the sins of humanity. He actually became sin so we could be seen as sinless. Every disease, every anger issue, every addiction, every evil desire from the past, present, and future were nailed to the cross so we could be set free. What we struggle with today was taken care of two thousand years ago. If Jesus is your personal Savior, you are FREE. Like, RIGHT NOW!

Since Mark was writing this Gospel to Roman Christians, many of whom were Gentiles, this Gospel is a great starting point for nonbelievers or new believers because it is written so Gentiles will understand it. It's the basics. It shows what Jesus did and what we are called to do. ■

DAY 8

▶ How do you think people reacted when God's voice came out of the heavens during the baptism of Jesus?

▶ What do you think it means to have your sins forgiven?

▶ What is the connection between someone being healed and their sins being forgiven, as we see in the story of the paralytic (Mark 2:1–12)?

▶ How did Jesus respond when He was questioned for doing work on the Sabbath (Mark 2:23–28)?

▶ How did Jesus set the demoniac free (Mark 5:1–13)?
What does that story teach us about demons?

▶ Why do you think Mark focused on demons in so many of his
stories?

▶ Why wasn't Jesus as accepted in His hometown (Mark 6:1–6)?

▶ What did Jesus tell the disciples to do if they were not accepted
in a new town (Mark 6:11)?

DAY 10

▶ The first eight chapters of Mark are all about healings, miracles, and casting out demons. Which one of these stories was your favorite? Why?

▶ What did Peter do after Jesus foretold His death and resurrection? (Mark 8:32)

▶ What do you think Jesus meant when He said, "All things are possible for one who believes" (Mark 9:23)?

▶ Our key verse for this Gospel says, "For even the Son of Man did not come to be served but to serve, and to give His life as a ransom for many" (Mark 10:45). How did Jesus serve others? How does this inspire you to serve the people in your life better?

▶ Why do you think Jesus often responded to questions with a question?

▶ What do you think Jesus was implying when He told the parable of the tenants (Mark 12:1–12)?

▶ What was the lesson of the widow with the two copper coins (Mark 12:41–44)?

▶ What do you think was running through the disciples' minds when they were told of all the things to come?

DAY 12

▶ Why did the woman with the alabaster vial pour the perfume on Jesus's feet (Mark 14:3–9)?

▶ Peter denied Jesus three times. What do you think you would have done if you had been in Peter's situation?

▶ Jesus became sin so we could be completely set free. Anything you are dealing with today was taken care of two thousand years ago. Have you had a revelation of that concept yet? How does that change the way you live?

▶ Using concepts from Mark's Gospel, how would you evangelize to someone who is not a Christian? Remember, your audience won't have any understanding of the Old Testament, so give an overview of the gospel message in the most easy-to-understand way possible.

BLESSED are the **poor in spirit**,
for theirs is the KINGDOM OF HEAVEN.

BLESSED are those **who mourn**,
for they will be COMFORTED.

BLESSED are the **meek**,
for they will INHERIT THE EARTH.

BLESSED are those **who hunger and thirst for righteousness**, for they will BE FILLED.

BLESSED are the **merciful**,
for they will be SHOWN MERCY.

BLESSED are the **pure in heart**,
for they will SEE GOD.

BLESSED are the **peacemakers**,
for they will be called CHILDREN OF GOD.

BLESSED are those **who are persecuted because of righteousness**,
for theirs is the KINGDOM OF HEAVEN.

Matthew 5:3–10 NIV

The Beatitudes

Gospel of Luke

AUTHOR

The Gospel of Luke was written by a friend of Paul's named Luke. Two important things to note while studying this book as well as the book of Acts are that Luke was a doctor and also a Gentile.

DATE

This Gospel was likely written while Paul was imprisoned in Caesarea around AD 58 to 60 or during his Roman imprisonment in AD 60 to 62.

AUDIENCE

Luke addressed his Gospel to one man only: "most excellent Theophilus." So who in the world is Theophilus?

Scholars have made many different claims over the years as to who Theophilus was. Some say he was Paul's financial supporter, some believe he was Luke's master, and others believe that he was the Roman official or judge over Paul's trial.

I choose to agree with the last of the three main options. Luke does an amazing job of compiling all of his information from eyewitness interviews and then presents the case that neither Jesus nor Paul had any big issues with the Roman government. Also, Luke ends the book of Acts just before Paul's hearing—the same time that these writings would be presented to the judge.

REASON

As we just saw, this Gospel could have been written to win Paul's release so he could continue his journey of taking the gospel around the world. It is an amazing look at the gospel story from the perspective of a Gentile doctor who focused on the humanity of the Son of Man.

THEME

Christ is the Savior for the Gentiles too.

KEY VERSE

"For the Son of Man came to seek and to save the lost" (Luke 19:10).

When studying the four Gospels, the most important thing you can do is look at the stories through the eyes of the writer. In this case, Luke is likely writing to a Roman judge on behalf of his friend Paul. Therefore, the content is much more focused on how Jesus interacted with Gentiles, Romans, and women. Luke is a unique book in the sense that it includes many stories the other Gospel writers did not have because they weren't able to interview the right people. Luke was not present during the ministry of Jesus, so he had to get information from all of the eyewitnesses he could to piece together the proper narrative to secure Paul's release. That might be why the feel of this book seems a little different compared with the other Gospels. And Luke, being a doctor, approached Jesus from the perspective of the Son of Man. Hence the reason for Jesus's genealogy dating to the first man, Adam, through the line of Mary.

Luke found it important to spend time looking at the healing miracles of Jesus's ministry, not specifically to show the Romans that Jesus was God, but because, as a doctor, he probably was fascinated with them himself. The recordings are truly unbelievable to those who have not experienced or witnessed the power of God. Luke also looks more at the Holy Spirit and the power He produces through the natural man than the other Gospel writers. Luke and the book of Acts are more focused on being baptized in the Spirit and the actions of Jesus's disciples. Luke really is a Gospel for everybody, Jew and Gentile alike. Since Luke was a Gentile writing to a Gentile, this Gospel should be used as an evangelism tool with Gentiles. In my mind, it's probably the best one because Gentiles would understand it best.

Luke includes many important testimonies that we don't read about in the other Gospels. And all of these are used to teach us new things. Testimonies are among the greatest things that we can share with the world. They produce hunger. They produce connections. They can also boost faith in hopes that God will work for us in the same way He has for others. I believe Luke's Gospel will boost your faith and help see how good a Father we serve. ■

DAY 13

▶ While John the Baptist was still in Elizabeth's womb, he seemed to acknowledge a change in the spiritual realm even though Jesus also was not even born yet (Luke 1:39–45). How does this story affect your views on abortion?

▶ What does this show about children's discernment of the spiritual realm? How should this influence the way that we raise our children?

▶ What do you think was running through Joseph's mind when Mary told him she was pregnant? How do you think that changed when people began to prophesy over the child's future?

▶ When Jesus asked, "Did you not know that I must be in my Father's house" (Luke 2:49), what do you think He meant? Remember, he had not yet received the Holy Spirit, and this was around eighteen years before His ministry began.

▶ Jesus read Isaiah 61:1–2 in front of everyone at the synagogue (Luke 4:16–21) and finished by saying, "Today this Scripture has been fulfilled" (v. 21). Why do you think He read this specific text? And why did people respond the way they did?

▶ Many of those Jesus chose as His disciples probably were teens. What made Him choose teenagers instead of adults?

▶ How did Jesus respond when people complained about His dining with sinners (Luke 5:31–32)?

▶ Is it easy or hard for you to follow along with the parables Jesus told? Why do you think He explained things that way?

WEEKLY CHECK-IN & PRAYER

▶ What is the most important thing you learned this past week?

▶ How can you apply the teaching to your life?

▶ Write a short prayer for the week ahead.

▶ A group of women were some of Jesus's biggest supporters. How can we better serve the women of our communities today?

▶ What did you learn from the parable of the lamp (Luke 8:16–18)?

▶ How do you think the disciples first responded when Jesus gave them power and authority to perform miracles?

▶ Do you believe Jesus wants to use you to perform miracles today?

DAY 16

Read Luke 10–12

▶ How many people did Jesus send out in Luke 10? How were they feeling when they returned?

▶ Explain the main teaching of the good Samaritan story (Luke 10:30–37).

▶ How did Jesus teach His disciples to pray?

▶ What was the overarching theme from Jesus's discourse in Luke 12?

▶ What message did Jesus tell the Pharisees to pass on to Herod (Luke 13:31–35)?

▶ Is the gospel message for everyone? Give an example that supports your beliefs.

▶ What is the connection between the lost sheep, the lost coin, and the prodigal son (Luke 15)?

▶ What did you learn from the story of the rich man and Lazarus (Luke 16:19–31)?

DAY 18

▶ Why do you think only one leper returned to Jesus even though ten were healed (Luke 17:11–19)?

▶ What did Jesus compare His second coming to (Luke 17:22–37)?

▶ Our key verse for this Gospel says, "For the Son of Man came to seek and to save the lost" (Luke 19:10). Who are the "lost" Jesus was referring to?

▶ How well do you understand Jesus's second coming?

▶ Why do we celebrate communion (Luke 22:14–23)? What do the bread and wine represent?

▶ Notice how frequently Jesus left everyone to pray by himself. How does this inspire your prayer life?

▶ Why do you think it was hard for Jesus's followers to recognize him on the road to Emmaus (Luke 24:13–35)?

▶ Your testimony is one of the greatest things you can share with the world. Write out the key points of your testimony below.

Gospel of John

AUTHOR

The Gospel of John was written by the apostle John. He was the only disciple still alive, and times were changing before his eyes.

DATE

John wrote his Gospel sometime in the AD 80s before the persecution of Domitian began. This was his first book, with more to come before his death in around AD 98.

AUDIENCE

The Gospel of John was written to various churches around Asia Minor where he had influence. John was one of the elders in the church of Ephesus and was looked up to because of his experiences and wisdom.

REASON

John was written to show the audience that Jesus was both fully God and fully man. It was most likely used to provide information the other Gospels left out and to show more of a theological perspective on the life of Christ.

THEME

Jesus came to give eternal life because He is God.

KEY VERSE

"I came that they may have life and have it abundantly" (John 10:10).

OVERVIEW

The Gospel of John is ninety percent unique from Matthew, Mark, and Luke, which are called the *Synoptic Gospels*. John explores Jesus as the Son of God, including His pre-existent genealogy at the beginning of the Gospel.

Whereas the other Gospels looked at what Jesus did and said, John approaches his story from the inside by looking at how Jesus felt and who He was as a person. He made it a point to show that Jesus is fully human and fully divine at the same time. There was nothing that Jesus could do while on earth without help from the Father.

John had decades to map out his version of the gospel message, since he lived longer than the other disciples, and wrote his Gospel nearly thirty years later than the others did. He didn't want people wasting their time figuring out who Jesus was, so he put it all out on the table.

One thing to notice in all of John's books is that he writes in sevens. Seven is the number of perfect divinity and is a very important number in the Jewish faith. The top two things John focuses on in this Gospel are seven major miracles as well as seven "I am" statements. Those statements meant everything to John. ■

DAY 20

▶ How does each Gospel show Jesus's genealogy?

Matthew:

Mark:

Luke:

John:

▶ Isn't it amazing that the Creator of the universe came down to His creation to save it? Describe a time when you worked extra hard on a project and it didn't turn out as you had planned. How did that make you feel? How do you think God felt?

▶ Why do you think Jesus's first miracle was turning water to wine?

▶ The most popular verse in the Bible probably is John 3:16. Why do you think Jesus chose to speak it to one man at night instead of preaching it from a mountaintop?

▶ How is Jesus equal to God the Father (John 5:18–24)?

▶ Can you explain the Trinity?

▶ What did Jesus mean when He said, "I am the bread of life" (John 6:35)?

▶ What did Jesus mean when He said, "If anyone thirsts, let him come to me and drink" (John 7:37)?

WEEKLY CHECK-IN & PRAYER

▶ What is the most important thing you learned this past week?

▶ How can you apply the teaching to your life?

▶ Write a short prayer for the week ahead.

▶ What do you think Jesus wrote on the ground in front of the Pharisees and the adulterous woman (John 8:6)?

▶ Whom does society tell you not to talk to? What can you do to show them their worth?

▶ Jesus said, "The truth will set you free" (John 8:32). Do you believe that in today's society?

▶ Write a prayer about being more aware of your need for Jesus as a Shepherd.

DAY 23

▶ John focuses his Gospel on seven major miracles. List them below:

1. John 2:1–11

2. John 4:46–54

3. John 5:1–9

4. John 6:1–14

5. John 6:16–21

6. John 9:1–33

7. John 11:1–44

▶ What do all these miracles teach you about Jesus?

▶ John shares seven "I am" statements from Jesus. List them below:

1. John 6:35

2. John 8:12

3. John 10:9

4. John 10:11

5. John 11:25

6. John 14:6

7. John 15:5

▶ What is the role of the Holy Spirit?

▶ Jesus often spoke of the connection between joy and our faith. What role does joy play in your day-to-day faith? Where does joy come from? How can you increase it?

DAY 25

Read John 18–21

▶ Why do you think Judas betrayed Jesus?

▶ What was the significance of a crown of thorns?

▶ How did Jesus pass the Holy Spirit to His disciples (John 20:22)?

▶ Why did Jesus ask Simon Peter three questions in John 21:15–17?

I AM.

Acts

AUTHOR

As was the Gospel of Luke, the book of Acts was written by Dr. Luke, a friend of Paul. Luke shows that they were together during many of the travels and experienced the same miracles throughout.

DATE

This book was likely written around the same time as the Gospel of Luke, while Paul was imprisoned either in Caesarea around AD 58–60 or during his Roman imprisonment in AD 60–62.

AUDIENCE

Luke addresses Acts to Theophilus, as he did his Gospel.

Considering that Luke ends this book with Paul still awaiting trial, it seems as if the evidence for this being used as a document in the trial is increasing. As mentioned before, Theophilus might have been a Roman judge at the time.

REASON

The book of Acts possibly was used as a legal document to serve as a testimony on Paul's behalf. Thank goodness we still have it today because this book is a great historical account of the early Christian church.

THEME

The gospel message is for everyone, everywhere.

KEY VERSE

"But you will receive power when the Holy Spirit has come upon you, and you will be my witnesses in Jerusalem and in all Judea and Samaria, and to the end of the earth" (Acts 1:8).

OVERVIEW

The book of Acts is a historical look at the first thirty years of the early church and, in many cases, could be used as a model for missionary work around the world today.

It starts off with Jesus promising the disciples that they would receive the power of the Holy Spirit shortly and would end up preaching in Jerusalem, Judea, Samaria, and to the remotest parts of the earth.

Each one of those places represents another ring outside of their current sphere of influence. They were in Jerusalem, then right outside are Judea and Samaria, and then outside of that is everywhere else in the world. It can be used as a great plan for evangelism today no matter where you are located. You have your neighbor, your city, and then the rest of the world.

After instructing the disciples regarding the Holy Spirit, telling them that He was coming and was going to empower them, we see that Jesus ascended into heaven and left them with a hope to hold on to.

The followers of Jesus were then filled with the Holy Spirit, and the church was finally able to begin building itself up based on what they had been taught through Jesus's ministry. It was go time. It's safe to say that they were hit with quite a bit of resistance right off the bat. That seems to be the case any time the Holy Spirit moves in mighty ways, even today. ∎

DAY 26

Read Acts 1–4

▶ What is your church's mission statement for missions?

▶ Have you been filled with the Holy Spirit?

▶ Have you ever experienced the Holy Spirit moving around you? If so, what happened?

▶ Why do you think Peter and John were arrested?

▶ What are your thoughts on the Ananias and Sapphira situation (Acts 5:1–11)?

▶ What are your thoughts on using signs and wonders for evangelism purposes?

▶ Why do you think people were so upset about the spreading of the gospel message into new parts of the world?

▶ What did you learn from Stephen's defense in Acts 7?

DAY 28

▶ Why was the Scripture that the Ethiopian eunuch was reading so important (Acts 8:26–40)? And why was he confused?

▶ What do you think was going through Ananias's mind when the Lord told him to heal Saul, the man who was persecuting believers in Jerusalem?

▶ Saul went back to his hometown for nearly a decade to preach and build himself up before going on any missionary journeys. What about us? Do our hometowns see the fire in each of us? They need to see our changed life before the world will. How can you use Saul as an example regarding hometown missionary work, instead of just doing short-term mission trips every once in a while?

▶ What was the purpose of Cornelius's vision in Acts 10?

WEEKLY CHECK-IN & PRAYER

▶ What is the most important thing you learned this past week?

▶ How can you apply the teaching to your life?

▶ Write a short prayer for the week ahead.

DAY 29

▶ What are your thoughts on the death of Herod (Acts 12:20–23)?

▶ Do you think Saul dealt with any fear of what others thought of him during his first missionary journey? If he did, how do you think he overcame that fear?

▶ Why was Saul's name changed to Paul?

▶ Why do you think God used Paul, who was Jewish, as an evangelist to the Gentiles?

▶ What was the reason for the Jerusalem Council in Acts 15? What was the final consensus? What does that mean for us?

▶ Paul was blocked from going to Bithynia in Acts 16. Have you ever been "blocked" by the Holy Spirit from going somewhere? If so, what happened?

▶ Was there anything different between Paul's first, second, and third missionary journeys?

▶ Have you ever been mentored or discipled? Are you currently discipling anyone? How can you use this story as an example for evangelism?

DAY 31

▶ What was taking place in Ephesus (Acts 19:11–41)?

▶ How do you think missionary work was different back then versus now?

▶ Why was Paul seized in the temple (Acts 21:27–36)?

▶ Why was Paul moved to Caesarea (Acts 23:12–22)?

▶ Do you think King Agrippa believed Paul was innocent?

▶ What happened on the journey to Rome (Acts 27:14–44)?

▶ What happened to Paul while he was building up a fire on Malta (Acts 28)? Who did the natives of Malta think he was?

▶ Paul encountered struggle after struggle in spreading the gospel message. Have you dealt with any resistance yourself?

BONUS:
Paul's Missionary Journeys

Your task today is to fill in the blank maps on the next few pages with each route from Paul's three missionary journeys. ➜

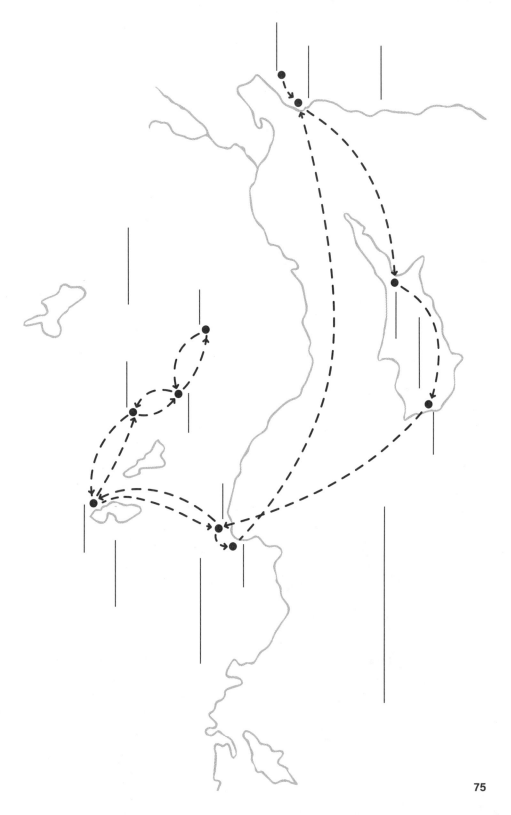

PAUL'S SECOND MISSIONARY JOURNEY

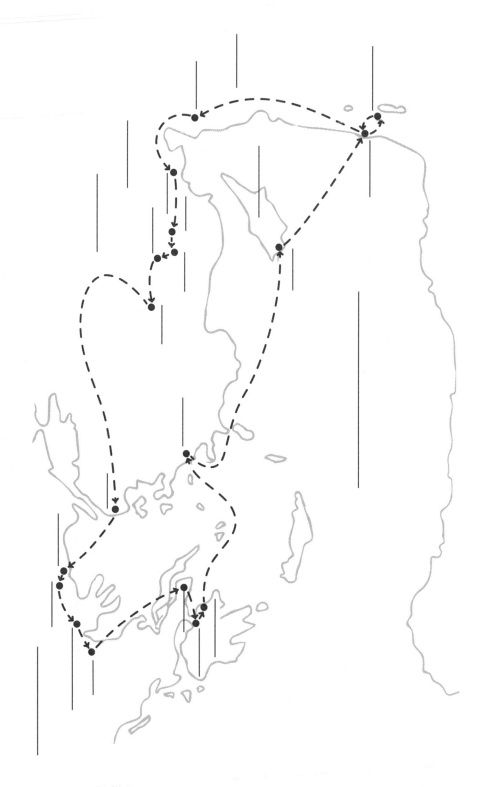

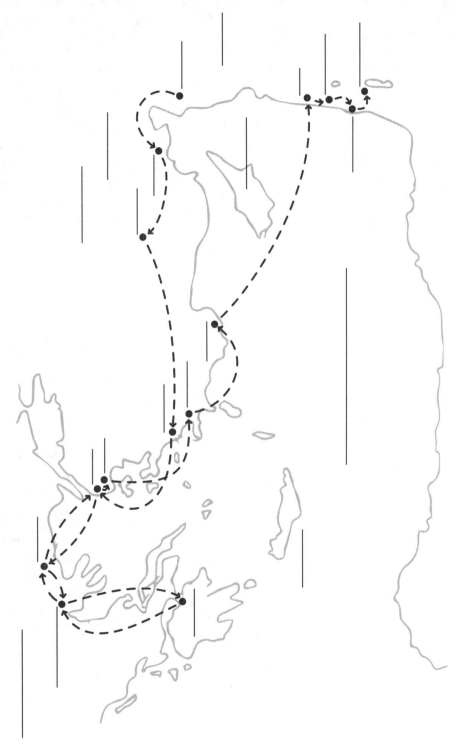

Romans

AUTHOR

The book of Romans was written by the apostle Paul.

DATE

Romans was written on Paul's third missionary journey around AD 55 to 56.

AUDIENCE

Paul was writing to a church that he had not visited before or personally known the leaders in Rome; we can conclude that from the entire chapter he used as a closing statement, to show that he knew the same people they did, which would help build credibility with them. There was a ton of tension in the Roman church between Jews and Gentiles at the time, with both making claims that they were in charge and that things would be done their way. Talk about a mess.

REASON

Romans was written to help resolve the tension between the Jews and Gentiles in Rome and to show that the groups were equal in God's sight. It was also written to explain the gospel as a whole, to be used for ministry advancement.

THEME

Basics of Christianity and Jew-Gentile relations.

KEY VERSES

"For I am not ashamed of the gospel, for it is the power of God to salvation for everyone who believes, to the Jew first and also to the Greek. For in it the righteousness of God is revealed from faith for faith, as it is written, 'The righteous shall live by faith'" (Romans 1:16–17).

Romans is a massive book. Not necessarily word-wise, but content-wise. It's so deep that it would take months to really dive into.

In short, Romans is the gospel. It's a book about grace and it's a book about redemption. This is God's plan for humanity. Therefore, it is extremely important that you take time to really understand this book.

Paul was one of the most influential Jews at the time, and he maintained a Jewish mindset even when reaching out to the Gentiles. Therefore, he understood his faith through the lens of a covenant relationship because that is what the Old Testament is heavily based on. We also must understand covenants to get what Paul is talking about.

So first off, how was a covenant cut, or made?

Well, to create a covenant was a serious thing. It started out with the kill. The two people entering into the covenant relationship began by finding a pure animal to sacrifice for the covenant ceremony. Once the animal had been selected, the two of them cut it in half along the spine, separating it into two sides. Remember, they didn't have electric saws back then like we have today, so at this point they were covered in blood, sweat, and maybe some tears. Completely and utterly exhausted.

The next step was the oath. They would lay out both sides of the animal, cut side open, facing each other, representing the two parties involved. They would each have a group of witnesses on their side. Then they would walk in a figure-eight pattern throughout the halves, repeating the terms of the covenant as they did so. After the terms were stated multiple times, they would take a rock and cut a large slice on their right hand followed by putting their hands together. Blood means life (see Leviticus 17:14). So the covenant parties' blood joining together symbolized their lives joining as well. The two became ONE.

Then they would rub dirt in their wound to create a scar as a visible reminder of the covenant. After all the rituals were complete, the witnesses from each side of the covenant had a large celebration together. And those in attendance would become responsible for holding the covenant parties accountable for their actions.

Like I said, to enter into a covenant was a major deal. It meant you died to yourself and there was no way out of it. Everything you did revolved around the terms of the covenant.

When God entered into a covenant with Abram in Genesis 15, He put him to sleep during the process and passed between the animal pieces Himself, employing fire and smoke. The reason Abram couldn't do the task was because he was still sinful, and God needed someone sinless to join Him. So God basically made a down payment to show that the covenant was unconditional and eternal. Two thousand years later we see that Jesus was the One without sin. Through Him we enter into that covenant when we are washed clean by His blood. When we come to Jesus, we are saying that we want to join in on His side of the covenant. We want to be a part of that covenant party now that it is complete. His representation allows us to be included in this whole thing. It's amazing!

Although we talk about the Old Testament and the New Testament, the Bible as a whole is one big covenant being fulfilled. Since we are believers in Christ, God sees Jesus when He looks at each of us. That is our new identity. We are His representatives here and now, spread out across the earth. This is the covenant we are part of. All of the church in one covenant, unified. We see throughout Paul's teaching that his main objective, besides preaching the gospel, was to unify the church. Each group had different views, but each was necessary for the church to function properly. Just like it is today. We get so caught up in which view is correct, when in reality, Jesus is coming back for His bride—singular. Not His non-denominational bride. Not His Pentecostal bride. Not His Lutheran bride. He is coming back for His ONE, spotless bride. We are all in this together.

Jesus is coming back for us, the church, and He loves His bride more than anything. So as one group of people is being used by God to perform miracles and is speaking in tongues, and another group is spending their time combing Scripture for answers on end-times theology, we need to love them both. Spirit and Scripture. Both are necessary. As I said earlier, and as you now know, Romans is a *massive* book. There is so much important information here that we need to spend time wrestling through. It is my prayer that you take time to continue studying this book at a later date and that God gives you a revelation of your new identity. ∎

▶ Define the word *gospel*.

▶ Our key verses include Romans 1:16, which reads, "For I am not ashamed of the gospel, for it is the power of God for salvation to everyone who believes, to the Jew first and also to the Greek." Have you ever been ashamed or quiet about your faith? If you have, why do you think that is?

▶ What is justification?

▶ Why did God give the Law to Moses (Romans 5:20–21)?

DAY 34

▶ Romans 6:12 (NIV) says, "Do not let sin reign." As good as that may sound, do you know how we can obey that command?

▶ What does it mean to be a saint? How does knowing that God now views you as a saint make you feel?

▶ What is sanctification?

▶ What does it mean to be glorified?

▶ What is God's plan for Israel?

▶ What statement about your identity as a child of God have you accepted that is really a lie from Satan?

▶ What are some ways we can bring the kingdom of God to earth today?

▶ Do you think the Roman church accepted this letter from Paul as truth? How do you think they responded?

POWER
LOVE
SOUND MIND

WEEKLY CHECK-IN & PRAYER

▶ What is the most important thing you learned this past week?

▶ How can you apply the teaching to your life?

▶ Write a short prayer for the week ahead.

1 Corinthians

AUTHOR

The author of both letters to the Corinthians was the apostle Paul.

DATE

First Corinthians was written between AD 55 and 56, while Paul was in Ephesus. Second Corinthians was written less than a year later from Philippi.

AUDIENCE

First and Second Corinthians were written to the church in Corinth and were later shared among other churches in the area. Corinth was a major party city in its time. We would compare it to Vegas today. It was a place of pleasure and indulgence. The Corinthians' focus was self-satisfaction. They weren't an easy bunch to deal with, but Paul was just the right guy for the job.

REASON

Paul was writing to help with church affairs based on reports from his friend Chloe's people and a letter sent by a group of Corinthians.

THEME

Love is the reason for everything.

KEY VERSE

"Let all that you do be done in love" (1 Corinthians 16:14).

OVERVIEW

From what we can gather in these two letters (1 and 2 Corinthians), we learn that Paul had actually written four letters to the church of Corinth, two of which we have and two that were lost.

The first problem Paul addressed was the division in the church. People disagreed on who they liked best, which leader they preferred, who they were baptized by, etc. Those divisions are very similar to the divisions we see in the church today. In America, there seems to be a different denomination on every street corner. And new ones keep arising. Mostly because of theological differences and new forms of interpretation.

One thing to note is that the Corinthians were highly influenced by a Greek mindset when it came to the role of their bodies. They thought spirituality was one thing and the body was another, one being good and the other evil. The two never crossed. Many believers today have the same Greek mindset when it comes to spiritual gifts that involve an outward act. We want to worship inwardly, but when it comes to a manifestation of the Spirit, some get freaked out.

So to break it down, there are four main views on spiritual gifts today.

Cessationist

Spiritual gifts were only for the early church and are not relevant today.

Continuationist

Spiritual gifts are for today, but the "sign" gifts need to be looked at and tested with caution.

Charismatic

Spiritual gifts are for every generation, and they should be practiced today. This view is limited by Scripture with no additions to the Word.

Hyper Charismatic

Spiritual gifts are for every generation, and contemporary revelations are equal to Scripture.

The main places in the Bible where we learn about spiritual gifts are 1 Corinthians 12–14, Romans 12, and Ephesians 4. Some people look at those lists and limit the gifts to them. But since we do not have a complete list, it can be fairly unclear as to what all of the gifts are, which, in turn, creates much disagreement in the church. One big mistake is to deny spiritual gifts altogether. Another mistake is to pick one and think that it's better than the others.

The spiritual gifts listed in those three main Scriptures are:

Romans 12: prophecy, service, teaching, encouragement, giving, leadership, and mercy.

Ephesians 4: apostleship, prophecy, evangelism, pastoring, and teaching.

1 Corinthians 12: word of wisdom, word of knowledge, faith, healing, miracles, prophecy, discernment, tongues, and interpreting tongues.

We have included a bonus section (after Day 38) for you to learn more about your spiritual gift(s) and see how God has made you unique in the body of Christ. ■

DAY 36

▶ Which denomination, if any, do you associate yourself with?

▶ Why do you think there is so much division in the church today?

▶ Have you ever given up on someone, in hopes of their learning on their own? If so, did they ever turn back to the truth? What does Paul describe as an immoral person in 1 Corinthians 5?

▶ What did Paul teach about marriage in 1 Corinthians 7?

▶ Paul speaks of eating things sacrificed to idols in 1 Corinthians 8. Can you think of any modern situations this teaching would apply to? What do you think Paul meant when he said, "Be imitators of me, just as I also am of Christ" (1 Corinthians 11:1 NASB)?

DAY 38

▶ Which view on spiritual gifts from the Overview section do you align with? Why?

▶ Which spiritual gift(s) do you think God has given you?
(See the following Bonus section for more information.)

▶ Have you heard anyone recite the famous love passage from 1 Corinthians 13? If so, where and when?

▶ How could you show love to those around you through your gifts?

HERE&NOW
HERE&NOW
HERE&NOW
HERE&NOW

BONUS:
Understanding Spiritual Gifts

Spiritual gifts are not to be confused with natural talent. Other important things to note:

- Every Christian has at least one spiritual gift.
- No Christian has every spiritual gift.
- Spiritual gifts can be abused.
- The Holy Spirit chooses which gifts each of us receive.
- God's will is not accomplished if love is not the main motivation behind the gifts.

Prophecy

Prophecy is the ability to speak truth into an individual's destiny and to reveal future events to the church in order to call for repentance or build them up. People with this gift can easily read others and "just know" things before they happen.

Teaching

Teaching is the ability to apply Scripture in an easy-to-understand way. People with this gift love to study and are focused on doctrinal application.

Giving

Giving is the ability to earn money in order to meet the needs of others in a cheerful manner. People with this gift are good at making money and like to give behind the scenes.

Mercy

Mercy is the desire to take care of those who are going through difficult times without expecting anything in return. People with this gift enjoy one-on-one serving and are able to sympathize naturally.

Service

Service is the ability to meet physical needs within the body of Christ and apply a spiritual significance to it. People with this gift like to work behind the scenes and get joy out of helping others.

Encouragement

Encouragement is the ability to motivate others on their faith journey. People with this gift are good counselors and can personally apply Scripture.

Leadership

Leadership is the ability to direct others in completing a God-given task of specific ministry work. People with this gift can clearly share a vision, and others gladly follow their lead.

Apostleship

Apostles are those who have a desire to be sent out to start churches and ministries in the local community and around the world. People with this gift are comfortable in other cultures and able to execute a specific vision.

Evangelism

Evangelists are those who can easily share the gospel with unbelievers and lead them to a personal relationship with Jesus Christ. People with this gift are very personable and convincing of the truth.

Wisdom

Wisdom is the ability to look at a situation and advise the best strategy for action based on the insight given. People with this gift can see various outcomes and can discern which action is the best to take.

Faith

Faith is the ability to have a confident belief that God will accomplish the impossible despite reality. People with this gift trust God completely and act in confidence.

Miracles

Those with the gift of miracles have the ability to be used as a vessel of God to reveal His power through supernatural acts that alter the natural realm. Miracles are most often used to authenticate the gospel message. People with this gift speak truth with confidence and have it authenticated.

Tongues

There are three types of tongues. One is a private prayer language (1 Corinthians 14:14–15). Another is the ability to speak out a divine message in a new language in order for the body of Christ to be built up. The third is an entire language as a gift, which is to be used for missionary work.

Pastoring

Pastors are those who guide, counsel, protect, and disciple a group of believers. Many times this gift is joined with the gift of teaching. People with this gift are great leaders and have a heart for discipleship.

Knowledge

Knowledge is the ability to understand the Word and make it relevant to the church or specific situations. This gift includes super-natural words of knowledge that are to be used in serving others. People with this gift are able to seek out truth in the Bible and typically have unusual insight into situations or a person's life.

Healing

Healing is the ability to be used as a vessel by God in order to cure sickness and restore health. People with this gift are able to demonstrate the power of God through prayer, the laying on of hands, or a spoken word.

Discernment (Distinguishing of Spirits)

Discernment is the ability to perceive what is from God through the recognition of good and evil spirits. People with this gift can easily tell what is from God and what is counterfeit.

Interpreting of Tongues

Interpreting of tongues is the ability to translate a foreign language that the hearer doesn't know, whether it is an earthly language or a heavenly language. ■

• • •

▶ Describe a time when you feel that God used you, whether you knew it involved your spiritual gift or not.

▶ What is the purpose of spiritual gifts? (1 Peter 4:10–11)

▶ Can you think of a way to exercise your gift(s) to grow it/them?

CHU

RCH

2 Corinthians

AUTHOR
The author of both letters to the Corinthians was the apostle Paul.

DATE
First Corinthians was written between AD 55 and 56, while Paul was in Ephesus. Second Corinthians was written less than a year later from Philippi.

AUDIENCE
The two letters were written to the church in Corinth and were later shared among other churches in the area. Corinth was a major party city in its time. We would compare it to Las Vegas today. It was a place of pleasure and indulgence. The Corinthians' focus was self-satisfaction. They weren't an easy bunch to deal with, but Paul was just the right guy for the job.

REASON
Second Corinthians was written by Paul as a defense of himself in response to a group of apostles challenging his authority and ministry. He wanted to encourage the church in their offering for Jerusalem and to remind them of their victory in Christ.

THEME
Victory in Christ.

KEY VERSE
"But thanks be to God, who in Christ always leads us in triumphal procession, and through us spreads the fragrance of the knowledge of him everywhere" (2 Corinthians 2:14).

While the first letter to the Corinthians dealt with practical issues within the church, the second letter deals with personal insults that forced Paul to stand up for himself. We know that a group of apostles came into Corinth once Paul left, and they tried to take over by building themselves up and pushing Paul down. We don't know who they were exactly, but the content suggests they were Jewish.

Some of the attacks on his character were that he wasn't bold enough, that he didn't care for the Corinthians since he was in a different city, that he wasn't a good speaker, and that he wasn't even qualified to be teaching them. The group of antagonistic apostles knew that if they successfully attacked Paul, his message would be thrown out as well. Paul does a good job of handling himself in such a crazy situation. He begins the letter in a sincere way and encourages them in their walk.

Around chapter 9 he gets a little upset, though, and starts to attack them for going against his teaching. Sometimes a little heat is necessary. Right in the middle of his encouragement and defense, Paul includes a large section on collecting money to give to the poor in Jerusalem. It's a quick pivot that is worth mentioning. We know from the past that Paul has a major heart for the poor, so that makes sense, but it does seem a little random. However, the Corinthians knew the importance of love, considering the whole chapter on it in his previous letter to them.

These apostles at Corinth weren't teaching love. They were attacking Paul and focusing on the negative instead. Paul knew that if he focused on loving others through donating to the poor they would turn toward the truth. And this approach worked because we know that Paul's third visit to Corinth was a joyous one. Second Corinthians encourages believers to embrace the transformed life that values generosity and humility. ■

DAY 39

▶ Why do you think Paul was attacked by this group of apostles?

▶ Think of a time when someone attacked your character. How did you handle it?

▶ Would you act differently after growing in your relationship with Jesus?

▶ Do you make it a point to serve the disadvantaged in your community?

▶ What are some ways you can better serve the underprivileged?

▶ Do you tithe to your local church? Why or why not?

▶ In what ways can you grow in generosity and humility?

NO OTHER NAME

—

JESUS

▶ Which characteristic of Paul's do you most desire to grow in?

▶ Have you ever had to defend your faith?

▶ What do you think Paul's "thorn in the flesh" was?

▶ In what ways can you test yourself to see how you are growing in your faith (2 Corinthians 13)?

Galatians

AUTHOR

The letter to the Galatians was written by the apostle Paul. He is the perfect person to write on the topic of freedom from the Law because of his past as a fully devoted Jew and a Pharisee. He knew about freedom in Christ alone more than anyone.

DATE

The dating of Galatians is highly debated. Some people believe that it was written early on as the first book in the New Testament, around AD 48, while others put the writing at around AD 55.

If Paul was writing to northern Galatia from Ephesus, the later date would make the most sense. On the other hand, if Paul was writing to southern Galatia from Antioch, the earlier date, before the Jerusalem Council, would fit better.

AUDIENCE

Whether you believe Galatians was written to the northern or southern part, we can agree that it was written to the churches of Galatia.

REASON

Paul was teaching the Galatians to be free from the Law because there were Judaizers and false teachers telling them otherwise.

THEME

Freedom through Christ alone.

KEY VERSE

"For freedom Christ has set us free; stand firm therefore, and do not submit again to a yoke of slavery" (Galatians 5:1).

The book of Galatians is much more negative compared with most of Paul's other letters because of how serious he is about being set free from the Law. There is no joking around with him on that matter. Freedom is everything. The Jewish people were strangling themselves with the Law. There was no way to fulfill it perfectly, but they still did their best to gain God's approval.

The most important ritual for a Jewish male was to become circumcised. It is a commandment from God! In Jewish culture it was mandatory then, and still is today. Paul is showing them that they no longer need to be circumcised to be saved, because Jesus's blood was the fulfillment of the circumcision covenant. Paul's main focus is showing the Jewish people that there is truly nothing they can do physically to become saved. It's all about grace.

They didn't get it, though, because for their entire lives the idea of having to work for salvation had been drilled into their heads. So the main issue we are dealing with here is whether salvation is received by faith or works. Paul is saying that it is by faith alone. A love like that was incomprehensible to the Jews. Quite frankly, it's incomprehensible to most believers today, many of whom still believe that going to heaven is about being a good person. That's a risky subject if you ask me. Because then I would have to ask this question: How good do you have to be to go to heaven? What's the measurement? We can never be good enough.

The gospel is truly scandalous. God's love doesn't make sense to the normal individual, but once you understand the gift is freely given, it makes it easier to accept it. Galatians 2:20 says, "I have been crucified with Christ. It is no longer I who live, but Christ who lives in me. And the life I now live in the flesh I live by faith in the Son of God, who loved me and gave himself for me."

I've learned that people crave simple plans. They want a checklist of things to follow to ensure their reward will come, which just so happens to be a similar mindset in many churches today. They want to know what they can and cannot do in order to one day go to heaven. Guess what, it's not all about one day getting to heaven. When you become a new creation, the focus of your life should shift to bringing heaven here, now. But for some reason, many denominations struggle with that understanding and provide the consumer with their desire for a simple plan instead.

Following rules to get into heaven is a great business model; it's just far from the truth because with it an actual relationship with Christ is put on the back burner or never even taught in the first place. Instead of getting so caught up in what we should and shouldn't do, I believe that we need to redirect our attention to our identity in Christ and who God says we are. Galatians 4:6–7 says, "And because you are sons,

God has sent the Spirit of His Son into our hearts, crying, 'Abba! Father!' So you are no longer a slave, but a son, and if a son, then an heir through God."

Because of what Jesus did, you are an heir to the throne and have received the same inheritance Jesus received. This. Is. HUGE. That means God blesses YOU the same way He blessed His Son, JESUS. With salvation, providing for our needs, understanding the Father's heart, joy, gifts, communication with God, answered prayers, etc. Our inheritance was already paid for, so God is literally just waiting for you to accept it. He gets joy out of blessing you. So take it in!

Some people may be wondering what it means to accept the blessing of the Father. It's as simple as asking Him for it and accepting your new identity. You are royalty. You are a son or daughter of the living God. LEGALLY. No ifs, ands, or buts. So look at yourself that way. Maybe you need to tell yourself that every day while looking in the mirror until it sticks. Seriously, DO IT. Your Father loves you and wants to bless you. New identity brings new fruit. ■

▶ What do you think Paul meant when he said it was no longer he who lived, but rather Christ who lived in him? How can you apply that to your own life?

▶ What rules do you see Christians placing on themselves today?

▶ How have you seen God's blessing on your life?

▶ What are the nine characteristics of the fruit of the Holy Spirit (Galatians 5:22–23)? What areas of the fruit do you need to improve on? What can you do to become better in those areas?

FISHERS OF MEN

WEEKLY CHECK-IN & PRAYER

▶ What is the most important thing you learned this past week?

▶ How can you apply the teaching to your life?

▶ Write a short prayer for the week ahead.

Ephesians

AUTHOR

The letter to the Ephesians was written by the apostle Paul.

DATE

Paul likely wrote Ephesians around AD 60 to 62, during his Roman imprisonment. It can be assumed that Paul wrote from there because he was on house arrest while in Rome, which meant that he had the freedom to preach, and his friends were still able to visit him.

AUDIENCE

Paul wrote this letter to the church at Ephesus in Asia Minor, and it was probably to be used as a circulatory letter to all of the churches in the area. Ephesus was a rough city. It was saturated with idol worship, and the people there would do anything possible to acquire salvation. Even so, the Ephesian church had a strong foundation.

REASON

The reason Paul wrote this letter was to teach them about identity and to show them how to stand firm by loving one another in their current culture.

THEME

Walking in your new identity.

KEY VERSE

"For we are his workmanship, created in Christ Jesus for good works, which God prepared beforehand, that we should walk in them" (Ephesians 2:10).

OVERVIEW

After his greeting, Paul begins Ephesians by saying, "Long before he laid down earth's foundations, he had us in mind, had settled on us as the focus of his love, to be made whole and holy by his love. Long, long ago he decided to adopt us into his family through Jesus Christ. . . . He wanted us to enter into the celebration of his lavish gift-giving by the hand of his beloved Son" (Ephesians 1:3–6 MSG).

There is so much about our new identity in this little section alone! We have been adopted. We are to be made whole and holy. God's desire is to bless us. Those are all amazing things! Paul also uses the word *predestination* in describing us, which is a highly debated concept today. To predestine means to "determine (an outcome or course of events) in advance by divine will or fate."* There are two main views on predestination: Calvinism and Arminianism.

Calvinism includes the belief that we were chosen for salvation. God chooses who He wants to be in the kingdom, and all of life is worked out in order for His plan to come to fruition. Calvinists preach largely that everything in life happens for a reason.

In Arminianism or Wesleyanism, on the other hand, the belief is that we were chosen to be in God's kingdom. In this view, your faith is conditioned upon that, and your future destiny is based on your actions now. Those in this school of thought believe in free will but hold that once you have chosen to follow God, He has a predestined plan for your life. You can find out more about each view and make up your mind.

Ephesians is all about identity and spiritual warfare. Spend time noticing what he says about you, the reader, as you are a child of God. There is so much power and authority behind you that allows you to walk in God's plan for your life, instead of in what the world tells you to do or how to act. ■

---

*"predestine," *The Oxford Pocket Dictionary of Current English*, *Encyclopedia.com,* May 27, 2023, https://www.encyclopedia.com/humanities/dictionaries-thesauruses-pictures-and-press-releases/predestine.

DAY 43

Read Ephesians 1–6

▶ What does it mean to be made whole and holy?

▶ Which citizenship do you tend to view life from? A heavenly one? Or earthly? What are some things you can do to have more of a heavenly perspective?

▶ Have you ever dealt with spiritual warfare before? How can you ruin the works of the devil in your daily life?

▶ List the armor of God.

1.

2.

3.

4.

5.

6.

YOU GOT THIS
DON'T GIVE UP
KEEP GOING
I BELIEVE IN YOU
GOD'S GOT YOU

Philippians

AUTHOR
The letter to the Philippians was written by the apostle Paul.

DATE
Philippians likely was written around AD 61–62, toward the end of Paul's Roman imprisonment.

AUDIENCE
Paul was writing to the church in Philippi, which consisted mainly of a Gentile audience.

REASON
Philippians was written to warn the Philippians about false teachings that were creeping into the church and to encourage them to remain joyful in the Lord.

THEME
Joy in the Lord.

KEY VERSE
"Rejoice in the Lord always; again I will say, rejoice" (Philippians 4:4).

OVERVIEW

When looking at the Bible as a whole, the letter to the Philippians can be put in the category of *prison epistles*, alongside Ephesians, Colossians, and Philemon. Philippians was written after those three as Paul was ending his stint under Roman house arrest.

Paul had been told of issues among the Philippians by a gentleman named Epaphroditus, who was sent to Paul as somewhat of a housekeeper. This letter was a response to those issues and a promise that Epaphroditus would be sent home soon.

Early on in Paul's letter we get the infamous quote, "For to me, to live is Christ and to die is gain" (1:21). Paul is eager to go to heaven, but he's willing to stay because he loves people that much. Obviously, God wants him to stick around since he came so close to death on all of his journeys but never ended up dying. The biggest problem that the Philippians were dealing with was disunity within the church. Pride and jealousy were seeping into the areas of blessings and spiritual gifts. Some people were becoming jealous that they weren't receiving the same spiritual gifts as others, and that caused resentment among the group.

In the letter, Paul tells them to "join in imitating me" (3:17) because he was so much like Christ. He's not being cocky, as we would assume after reading that; he's just confident in who he is. He's imitating Christ, so that's what the Philippians should be doing. He's their tangible evidence of someone following Christ and properly walking in their new identity. As you know, Paul spent a lot of time in jail. People weren't too keen on his causing a scene in their city by talking about Jesus and disrupting business, so they would just send him off in shackles. Wouldn't you think after the first or second time that he'd quiet down a little bit? He didn't. He just brushed off his shoulder and kept on going. If it weren't for his prison sentences, then we wouldn't have the prison epistles, so I'm alright with it.

Honestly, what else would you do while in prison but write motivational letters to churches telling them to keep doing the same thing you're currently in jail for? Duh. It's wild, though, because this whole letter is filled with his constant joy, and he mentions a ton of times that they should rejoice because life is wonderful.

Paul believed that no matter what happened in his life, it would all be used for a higher purpose. If he was in jail, he could work with it. If he was having the worst day ever in a normal person's life, he could work with it. Paul was joyous no matter what happened in his life because he knew God was always looking out for him. And so that's where I'm at. You want to know how I can have a good day every day, no matter what I'm put through? It's because my joy comes from knowing Jesus. That's it. Nothing more, nothing less. ■

DAY 44

▶ What does the statement "to live is Christ" mean? How can you go about doing that?

▶ What does it mean to rejoice always? In which areas of your life do you struggle with remaining joyful?

▶ What does Paul tell us to think about in Philippians 4:8? How can you obey that personally?

▶ In what ways can changing your outlook on life help you navigate your current circumstances?

Rejoice

Pray

~~Complain~~

Be thankful

Colossians

AUTHOR

The letter to the Colossians was written by the apostle Paul.

DATE

Paul wrote Colossians at the same time as Ephesians and Philemon, around AD 60–61, during the beginning of his Roman imprisonment.

AUDIENCE

This letter was written to the church at Colossae, which was made up mostly of Gentiles.

REASON

Colossians was written to correct some false teachings that were distorting the Colossians' view of Jesus, to show them the full deity of Christ, and to show their fullness in Christ.

THEME

Fullness in Christ.

KEY VERSES

"For in Him all the fullness of Deity dwells in bodily form, and in Him you have been made complete, and He is the Head over every ruler and authority" (Colossians 2:9–10 NASB).

As we learned when looking at Philippians, Paul was under Roman house arrest at the time of this writing. During house arrest, he could have visitors and live somewhat freely, all the while chained to a Roman soldier.

A man named Epaphras, who was part of the church in Colossae, reported to Paul that things were going badly. Paul had no formal authority over the Colossians, but he did his best to redirect their focus to understand their new identity in Christ. A large portion of Colossians matches the content in Ephesians, so we don't have too many new topics to look at in this book. It also helps that Paul writes to them in a very straightforward way so they will understand it.

False teachings were taking place among the church in Colossae because they felt there was no way Christianity could be so simple. So they made it hard. They added different rules and regulations to their doctrine, which took away from the simplicity of the gospel and formed a religion instead. In reality, Jesus came to save us from religion. The true gospel is Jesus plus nothing. But people make countless additions.

That's what makes Colossians so relevant to us today. When we spend our time adding tasks to the gospel, it causes Jesus to lose His authority in our lives. He is really the be-all and end-all. He is all we need. God is looking for people who will live in the simplicity of the gospel and let the work of Jesus reign supreme in their lives. He wants to work with you on creating wholeness in every situation and every relationship you're involved in. He desires a relationship, not religion.

One of the distinct characteristics of Colossians is that it is a great example of Christology, which is the study of Christ. Paul gives an in-depth analysis of who Christ was and is, and how He relates to us. We have looked at it multiple times, but when we come into Christ, we become a completely new creation. Our old self is gone, and our new self has taken over. The past has LITERALLY been forgotten because God loves you SO MUCH. There is no need to dwell in the old anymore. Christ is now living inside of us, and He wants to influence the lives of everyone around us.

Sharing God's love and the good news about Jesus are our main purpose now that we have accepted it. You may be the only Christian that the people around you come in contact with today, and Jesus loves them just as much as He loves you. So share it. ∎

DAY 45

Read Colossians 1–4

▶ What do you add to your faith out of habit or from church pressure that may distract you from your relationship with Jesus?

▶ What does Paul mean by "put on the new self" (Colossians 3:1–17)?

▶ In what ways has your identity been changed now that you are a follower of Jesus?

▶ What are your favorite ways of sharing the love of Christ?

HOLD FIRMLY TO THE TRUTH

1 and 2 Thessalonians

FIRST LETTER

AUTHOR

The two letters to the Thessalonians were written by the apostle Paul. Silas and Timothy were present during the writing, but the doctrine was all his.

DATE

Paul wrote the first letter to the Thessalonians around AD 50–51 while in Corinth, and the second letter was sent just a few months later.

AUDIENCE

The Thessalonians were a group of new believers who didn't get much formal training from Paul. They were likely predominantly Gentile and had been brought up under pagan worship. We know that they were already being persecuted for their faith and were being sent false letters that claimed to be from Paul in order to sway them from the truth.

WHERE WAS THESSALONICA?

Thessalonica was at the northernmost part of the Aegean Sea, and it was also along the Egnatian Way on land. It was in one of the best spots possible for starting a church in hopes of its message being spread all over the Greco-Roman world. Business flourished there because of its location. It was definitely the place to be.

Paul visited Thessalonica on his second journey after being led there by the Holy Spirit. We saw that story in Acts when the Holy Spirit blocked Paul and his companions from going to Asia, but Paul saw a man in his dream who urged him to go to Macedonia. Thessalonica was the capital city of Macedonia during the Roman empire.

A little while after establishing the church in Thessalonica, Paul was working in Corinth when he received a support letter from the Thessalonians. Paul's first letter to the Thessalonians is in response to their gift.

REASON

Paul wrote to encourage them to press on in their faith, to not listen to the false accusations against him, and to keep working hard until the Second Coming.

THEME

In expectation of Christ.

KEY VERSE

"Now may the God of peace himself sanctify you completely, and may your whole spirit and soul and body be kept blameless at the coming of our Lord Jesus Christ" (1 Thessalonians 5:23).

OVERVIEW

Paul starts off by commending them for living out their faith so well. You can tell he is happy with the way that they have been doing things. Paul tends to be a professional motivator. He knows just what to say to get people to progress in their faith. And it works almost every time because they know that he truly cares about them and does it from a place of love. Paul also focuses more on their holiness than on themselves.

The Thessalonians are taught to excel in love toward one another and to work hard so they wouldn't be in need of anything. He writes in 1 Thessalonians 4:10–12, "We urge you, brothers, to do this more and more, and to aspire to live quietly, and to mind your own affairs, and to work with your hands, as we instructed you, so that you may walk properly before outsiders and be dependent on no one." Yikes. For some reason, work is a topic rarely discussed within the church today. In Genesis 3, God says that because of the Fall, we will be forced to work, and it won't be fun.

Paul is continuing on with the same statement here. He is saying that if you are able to work, you should be making your own money and taking care of your responsibilities, not expecting to live off of others' money.

We can partner with God in building up people He loves. That goes for believers and unbelievers alike. Encouraging each other's gifts increases our confidence in what God gave us. It can also allow us to push boundaries and grow in our own spiritual life.

Chapter 5 is packed with a bunch of unrelated goodies Paul wanted to tell them before closing out the letter. He says that it is God's will for us to rejoice, pray, and be thankful at all times (vv. 16–18). Then he says not to quench the Spirit (v. 19) and not to despise prophetic utterances, but to examine them carefully (vv. 20–21). Both are very important things.

Many times we can be extra skeptical about prophecies, especially in the US, because they aren't a commonly taught subject. But the New Testament consistently shows that prophecy is a major part of the Christian life. That sure is something to pray about. Let God speak to you about His heart on this subject.

SECOND LETTER

REASON
Paul wrote to comfort the Thessalonians in the affliction and false teaching regarding the Second Coming.

THEME
Comfort until the Second Coming.

KEY VERSES
"Since indeed God considers it just to repay with affliction those who afflict you, and to grant relief to you who are afflicted as well as to us, when the Lord Jesus is revealed from heaven with his mighty angels" (2 Thessalonians 1:6–7).

OVERVIEW

Second Thessalonians is far different from Paul's first letter to the Thessalonians, even though they were written only a few months apart. Paul now seems to be very distant from them and upset over something that was reported to him shortly after the first letter was sent.

He starts off by complimenting them, but quickly gets into the heavy stuff. The Thessalonians had received a false letter seeming to be from Paul saying that the Second Coming was just around the corner so there is no need to work or press on in their faith anymore. The sad thing is that many people believed it.

Paul goes on to say that it couldn't be close because the man of lawlessness had yet to make himself known, so they had awhile. Paul continues with his thoughts on work from the first letter and encourages the Thessalonians again to keep at it. He goes so far as to tell them not to give Christians food if they aren't willing to work (3:10).

A lot of the Thessalonians were being lazy. And I see that a lot today, not necessarily in the area of work, but definitely in the areas of evangelism and prayer. This should be anything but a time to slow down! We should be ramping up our evangelism and prayer lives more than ever if we truly believe that the Second Coming is approaching.

God created us to work alongside Him. We aren't His robots. He actually desires us to be creative with Him and co-labor throughout the day, whatever that looks like for your situation—it's different for everyone. It's such a privilege to get to work with our Father every day.

It's interesting to note that what are likely the first two letters written in the New Testament were about the Second Coming. There has been a lot of talk about the topic lately and many people are wondering if it will happen during their lifetime. That would obviously be a GREAT thing for us, but a TERRIBLE thing for those around us who have yet to be saved. And it's our responsibility to share the gospel with them. ■

▶ Would you consider yourself a hard worker? Do you view work as if you're working for the Lord?

▶ Do you think the antichrist will rise up during your lifetime? Why or why not?

▶ Do you have a good enough understanding of hell to make you want to evangelize? Or are you fine knowing that some of the people around you will go there?

▶ List three people you want to evangelize to this year and outline a short plan for encouraging each of them.

1 and 2 Thessalonians

1 and 2 Timothy

FIRST LETTER

AUTHOR
The two letters to Timothy were written by the apostle Paul.

DATE
First Timothy was written around AD 64–66, likely from Macedonia.

AUDIENCE
Paul wrote this letter to Timothy, whom he loved so much that he considered him his own son. He also trusted Timothy immensely and encouraged him to always press on through his timidity.

REASON
Paul wrote to encourage Timothy amidst opposition from false teachers and to instruct him on leadership within the church.

THEME
Leadership roles inside of the church.

KEY VERSES
"I hope to come to you soon, but I am writing these things to you so that, if I delay, you may know how one ought to behave in the household of God, which is the church of the living God, a pillar and buttress of the truth" (1 Timothy 3:14–15).

SECOND LETTER

DATE
Second Timothy was written around AD 67 just before Paul's martyrdom. Paul was back in prison in Rome at the time.

AUDIENCE
Timothy, Paul's "beloved child" (2 Timothy 1:2), was still in Ephesus and was dealing with false teachers.

REASON
This is Paul's final epistle, in which he hands over the ministry responsibilities to Timothy.

Paul encourages him to have sound doctrine and to stand strong against opposition that will come his way.

THEME
Finish strong, Timothy!

OVERVIEW

First Timothy, Second Timothy, and Titus all were written by Paul during his final missionary journey and the beginning of his second Roman imprisonment. They are known as the *pastoral epistles* because Timothy and Titus were in pastoral positions in different cities, and Paul is teaching them how to get their people in line. He knew how important order in the church was for effective evangelism. And we all know Paul's thoughts on evangelism: It was everything. Even though they are called the pastoral epistles, it was neither Timothy's nor Titus's job to remain in each location as the pastor. Paul sent them to set things straight, but the main desire of his heart was for them to meet him in Rome before he was martyred.

Timothy was sent to deal with the leadership in Ephesus, but we know that he was a timid man, meaning the task was far outside of his comfort zone. Titus, on the other hand, was sent to Crete to deal with the church as a whole (elders and members), but he was strong and self-sufficient, which made Paul's job much easier. Not only were these letters used as motivation and direction, but Paul knew that they would also be used as credentials to prove the authority of Timothy and Titus.

From these letters and also from the book of Acts, we know that Timothy had a

Greek father and a Jewish mother. His father may not have been around much, so Timothy had a Jewish upbringing by his mom and grandma. In Acts 16, Paul urged Timothy to get circumcised, not for a religious purpose, but to be allowed into the synagogue for evangelism purposes.

Paul sent Timothy to sort out the issues in Ephesus that could not be handled through a letter. Not only were things bad in Ephesus, but Christians in Rome were facing an alarming level of persecution by Nero.

Paul was in prison, and he knew his martyrdom was right around the corner. Therefore, it was time to hand things over to Timothy. That's the reason why Paul is so adamant about Timothy continuing on in the faith and persevering until his mission is complete.

Time and again, Paul had seen people backtrack in their faith when persecution began to heat up. Timothy was not going to be one of them, not if Paul had anything to do with it. Paul's advice was to keep pressing on, no matter what happened. He knew it would all be worth it in the end even though Timothy was beginning to lose hope.

Timothy was timid, but his calling overpowered what people said about him. The same thing goes for you today. Typically, your calling is something impossible in the eyes of society, but it is always in line with God's will. Good thing for you that our God is the God of the impossible, and He almost always calls the unqualified.

You aren't the first and you definitely aren't the last. Just as Paul is telling Timothy to press on through the impossibilities, he is telling us the same thing. God likes to show off through our lives. But in so many cases, we fail to recognize that because we have such a worldly mindset. If you keep your eyes on God and acknowledge that He wants to use you for His divine tasks, you will soon realize what a privilege it is to work for your Father every day. ∎

▶ Do you know anybody who was a strong believer but ended up leaving their faith? What were their reasons?

▶ How do you stay strong when times get tough?

▶ What characteristics do you think good leaders have?

▶ Do you sense God calling you to do something impossible by human standards? What is it? What is stopping you?

1 and 2 Timothy

VEN

Titus

AUTHOR
The apostle Paul wrote this letter to Titus.

DATE
Paul wrote to Titus at the same time as First Timothy, around AD 64–66 while in Macedonia.

AUDIENCE
Titus was Paul's representative, and he didn't need to have his hand held. He was strong and followed directions well, always finding a way to accomplish the given task. Paul had sent him to the island of Crete to get the members of the church there in line. Unlike Timothy, Titus was fully Greek and an uncircumcised believer.

REASON
Paul quickly touches on leadership and then instructs Titus how to teach godly living among members of the church in Crete.

THEME
Sound doctrine is everything.

KEY VERSE
"Therefore rebuke them sharply, that they may be sound in the faith" (Titus 1:13).

OVERVIEW

Notice how different the tone is in the letters to Timothy and Titus. Whereas Timothy was very timid, Titus was strong and self-sufficient. Paul knew that he could send Titus to perform a task, and he would find a way of getting it done. Titus didn't need his hand held, and Paul knew it. He dropped him off on the island of Crete and had him get to work.

Crete was a bad place. It was similar to parts of Las Vegas today. Immorality at its worst. Titus was put in the thick of it, and although he was kind of in over his head, that didn't stop him from giving it a shot.

Paul wrote to encourage Titus and to help him deal with the immorality all around him. Just as he did with Timothy, Paul told Titus what to do with the leadership, but his main focus was on the people, since false teachings were beginning to creep into the Cretans' doctrine. Paul teaches the members how to act to keep the entire church in line. He focuses on two things: character and truth, both of which must be present in all members. He emphasizes having a good character outside of the church and a solid foundation in Scripture.

Paul says that we are to adorn the gospel. Looking good to unbelievers is something that Paul addresses. Believers need to show unbelievers that what we have is better than what they have. We have the answers to all of life's problems. We have the Creator of the universe available 24/7. I believe that the church really needs to improve in this area. We have separated ourselves so far from society that we often have no idea what would draw unbelievers in. Society portrays us as prudish, boring, and hypocritical. Paul says that we must live up to what is good in society's eye and take that one step further. Our goodness and love should draw unbelievers in.

As we see in Timothy and Titus, having a strong foundation is the most important thing we can do as false teaching continues to infiltrate the church. We have to know our stuff. ■

Philemon

AUTHOR

The author of this letter to Philemon was the apostle Paul.

DATE

Paul wrote to Philemon at the same time as Ephesians and Colossians, around AD 60–61, during his Roman imprisonment.

AUDIENCE

The letter to Philemon was written to Philemon, but Paul also includes Apphia, Archippus, and their house church in Colossae, possibly to hold Philemon accountable for the content of the letter.

REASON

Paul wrote as an appeal for Philemon to forgive Onesimus for running away and to show that he was now useful in sharing the gospel.

THEME

Forgiveness, equality, and reconciliation in Christ.

KEY VERSE

"I appeal to you for my child, Onesimus, whose father I became in my imprisonment" (Philemon 10).

Philemon is the only personal letter of recommendation in the Bible. So what is going on here that makes this book part of Scripture?

Well, back in the day, slavery was much different from what it is today and has been in the more recent past. Whereas our views regarding modern slavery are all about de-humanization and brutality, being a slave in the Greco-Roman world could be a decent profession. Neither the conditions nor the wages were necessarily bad, and some scholars contend there were more slaves than there were free people. So here we have a man named Onesimus who was a slave of a man named Philemon. Onesimus had run away, most likely while he was out running an errand for a wealthy man named Philemon.

We don't know exactly what happened—some surmise he stole from his master, though Scripture does not say that—but we do know that the penalty for running away was death. Onesimus ran so far away that he wouldn't be found by Philemon. While he was in Rome he was introduced to Paul, who was on house arrest.

During their time together, Onesimus gave his life to Christ. Before Onesimus could go any further, Paul made him go back home and ask Philemon for forgiveness. Yikes. When you enter into life with Christ, it doesn't mean that you can run from your past. Yes, you are forgiven and have been wiped clean, but you also have the opportunity to make your past right by bringing wholeness to your relationships and situations.

The good thing about the story with Onesimus and Philemon is that Paul knew Philemon, so he could send a letter to him explaining the situation. But that didn't mean Onesimus was off the hook. His life was still in the hands of Philemon, since the consequence for a runaway slave was death.

On top of it all, Paul was making Onesimus hand-deliver the letter. He had to walk nearly fifteen hundred without knowing the outcome. This letter was literally life or death for him.

One of the coolest things about this story is that the name Onesimus means useful. By sending the slave back with this letter, Paul is saying that he will now live up to his name and be useful to Philemon, as he is to Paul. He's a completely new creation. He has a purpose now. But first things first, he needs to get his relationships right. We assume that Philemon handled it well because we still have the letter today.

Forgiveness isn't an easy thing, but it can be the one thing that changes your life. God has forgiven you of your past and has given purpose to your formerly useless life, just as we see here with Onesimus. ■

DAY 48

▶ What virtues does our culture associate with good people? How can we live those out?

▶ Ask God to point out anything in your life that might be holding you back from maturity, then write them down.

▶ What do you think was going through Onesimus's mind on his journey back to Philemon?

▶ Spend some time thinking about whether you need to make an Onesimus journey of your own. If you do, reach out and either ask for forgiveness or forgive someone. Write about the experience below.

Titus and Philemon

JESUS IS BETTER

Hebrews

AUTHOR

Nobody really knows who the author of Hebrews is, and, quite frankly, there are several possibilities: Luke, Paul, Barnabas, Apollos—even Priscilla and Aquila have been proposed. Understanding the content of the book is not based on your view of the authorship, so do not get hung up on trying to figure it out.

DATE

The book of Hebrews was most likely written around AD 64–65. The temple had yet to be destroyed, and Nero was just beginning his persecution of Christians.

AUDIENCE

The author of Hebrews directed his attention toward Hebrew believers who were turning their focus back to the religious nature of Judaism.

REASON

The book of Hebrews was written to show how Jesus and the New Covenant are superior to Judaism and the Law. The author also encouraged the Hebrew believers in their faith journey as they dealt with a new wave of persecution.

THEME

Jesus is better than Judaism.

KEY VERSE

"But in fact the ministry Jesus has received is as superior to theirs as the covenant of which he is mediator is superior to the old one, since the new covenant is established on better promises" (Hebrews 8:6 NIV).

OVERVIEW

Hebrews is not an easy book for many Gentile readers to get through because of their lack of Old Testament knowledge. As I have said, it is *crucial* to put yourself in the shoes of the reader as best you can; otherwise, your understanding of the context will fall short.

In chapter 1, the author displays Jesus as being perfect. He lists seven reasons He is better from the get-go (vv. 2–4), and we know that the number seven symbolizes divine perfection.

Later in that chapter, the writer's first main point in a further listing of Jesus's superiority is that Jesus is better than angels. What does that mean? It means that Jesus is a much better messenger between God and man than anything they had experienced in the past. Jews relied heavily on interaction with angels in order to know the heart of the Father. But we have the heart of the Father in human form, Jesus, giving us the opportunity to align our hearts with his. Also, as much as some angels may want to be as great as God himself—remember Satan—angels are not and will never be like God.

Then the author looks at Jesus as being better than Moses and Joshua (chapters 3 and 4), with the main focus on Moses. Moses was the be-all and end-all in Judaism. All Jews look to him as the definition of holiness and the image to strive after. Many times Moses was seen as being interchangeable with the Law because he was the one who received it from God.

Then we learn that Jesus is better than the Aaronic priesthood. The Old Testament is great for discovering what types of leadership did and did not work for the Israelites. When it came down to it, none of the leadership types the people desired ended up working well. They tried the leadership of priests, prophets, judges, and kings individually, but what they really needed was someone who could fill all of these roles. The Aaronic priesthood was birthed out of the holiness required under the Law. The Law was something to measure holiness against and, in reality, showed the people that a holy life was impossible without a savior. The Israelites' hope was to remain in their future Messiah. And until the Messiah came, life was going to be very difficult. The coming of Christ erased the need for the earthly priesthood because whereas the Law brought death, Christ brought life and life abundantly. Hallelujah!

Then we see that Jesus is better than the Old Covenant. The Old Covenant was inferior because it was never God's original intention. People couldn't live up to the 613 laws they were called to obey. They wanted to live a life that mimicked the surrounding societies, and peer pressure played a major influence. Time after time, God gave them what they wanted, but it was never enough. The Law and God's involvement weren't the issues. It was people's selfish desires and pride that made them stumble. They needed a foolproof way to be right with God. They needed Him to perform something miraculous. They needed a new covenant and a new nature.

The author of Hebrews makes it clear that focusing on religion will get you nowhere, while accepting the redemptive work of Jesus will give you eternal life and an abundant one here and now. Our job is to act in faith in response to what God calls us to do. ■

DAY 49

▶ From the beginning of this book, the author lists seven reasons why Jesus is perfect. List those seven things:

1. Hebrews 1:2b

2. Hebrews 1:2c

3. Hebrews 1:3a

4. Hebrews 1:3b

5. Hebrews 1:3c

6. Hebrews 1:4a

7. Hebrews 1:4b

▶ What characteristics make Jesus better than angels (Hebrews 2:9–18)?

▶ In what ways is Jesus better than Moses, as described in the text?

▶ How would you define unbelief (Hebrews 3:7–19)? What are some of the ways that you can help each other to continue believing?

WEEKLY CHECK-IN & PRAYER

▶ What is the most important thing you learned this past week?

▶ How can you apply the teaching to your life?

▶ Write a short prayer for the week ahead.

DAY 50

▶ Who is Melchizedek? Why was he important?

▶ In what ways is Jesus better than the Aaronic priesthood?

▶ How were people judged and served in the Old Covenant vs. in the New Covenant?

▶ List everything the author says Jesus is better than below:

1. Chapters 1–2:

2. Chapters 3–4:

3. Chapters 5–7:

4. Chapters 8–10:

▶ Who is your role model in Hebrews 11? What can you pull from their life as motivation to grow in your faith?

▶ On a scale of one to ten, where would you put your faith (with one being "I am a realist and don't think that God can use me to do the impossible" and ten being "If God says 'Jump', I JUMP")?

1   2   3   4   5   6   7   8   9   10

▶ What's holding you back from having greater faith?

▶ Make a plan of attack below for how you can better walk out your faith from here on out.

James

AUTHOR

The author of this epistle is James, the brother of Jesus.

DATE

There are two highly disputed timeframes for when the book of James was written.

The early view holds that James was written around AD 47–48, before the Jerusalem Council took place. Hence the reason for not using any of the content from the Jerusalem Council when disputing relevant topics.

According to the late view, however, James was written around AD 60–62, after the Jerusalem Council. This view would be taken if James was clarifying various misinterpretations of Paul's word.

AUDIENCE

James wrote to all the Jews who were scattered in the Dispersion that followed Stephen's death in Acts 8. It was a circulatory letter (meaning it was meant to be circulated among the churches), not addressed to a specific location.

REASON

James wrote to explain what fruit should be produced when we live an obedient Christian life and also stressed the need for wisdom from above.

THEME

Faith, works, and wisdom.

KEY VERSES

"So also faith by itself, if it does not have works, is dead. But someone will say, 'You have faith and I have works.' Show me your faith apart from your works, and I will show you my faith by my works" (James 2:17–18).

The book of James definitely could be called the Proverbs of the New Testament. It's known as *Wisdom Literature*, which means it is packed with content on how to live your life as a Christian. It's the least doctrinal type of writing, but it is the most practical for day-to-day living.

The five main topics James looks into are:

- Trials
- Faith and works
- The tongue
- Wisdom
- Wealth

Wisdom Literature doesn't typically follow an outline. James goes back and forth between topics with no obvious reasoning behind it. We are going to touch on the five main topics and see how they can each apply to today.

Trials

Christians know a lot about trials and tribulations. As we have looked at before, and will continue to see, being a new creation means that you are no longer worldly. You now belong to the kingdom of heaven instead of to the earth. Spiritual warfare tends to ramp up heavily when you begin walking in your new identity as a child of God, which creates trials and tribulations in your day-to-day life. A great description many believers use is that we are "in the world, but not of it," based on Jesus's words in John 15:19 and 17:14–16.

Our true home is in heaven now, making this earthly sod just a pit stop on the way home. One thing to realize when dealing with trials or spiritual warfare or persecution is that God may test you, but it is always Satan who tempts you. Testing is a way for you to grow in your faith, while tempting is done in hopes of making you fail. As you read in 1 Corinthians 10:13, "No temptation has overtaken you that is not common to man. God is faithful, and he will not let you be tempted beyond your ability, but with the temptation he will also provide the way of escape, that you may be able to endure it." In the Old Testament, God allowed Satan to *test* Job's faith in Him because He knew that Job was a faithful servant. Job was not given more than he could handle. So no matter what trial or tribulation you are put through, always keep your focus on Christ and allow Him to make you stronger in your faith.

Faith and Works

James approaches the topic of faith and works in a way that we do not see anywhere else in the Bible. Paul taught that salvation is through grace alone, not works, but he was talking about works from the Law, not good deeds. It is true that works do not create salvation, but it is also true that faith should result in good works. The Christian faith isn't just about saying that you believe in God, as many churches claim today. The Christian faith is about growth. It's about transformation. It's about sharing the love of Jesus through our actions.

The Tongue

The tongue is the most powerful part of your entire body. Because of that, it is also the most difficult piece to control. Our tongues have influence. Probably way more influence than we would like them to have. So small, yet so potent. In *The Message* translation, James 3:6 reads, "By our speech we can ruin the world, turn harmony to chaos, throw mud on a reputation, send the whole world up in smoke and go up in smoke with it, smoke right from the pit of hell." You don't hear much biblical teaching today on the tongue or the power of words, yet so many people struggle in that area.

Wisdom

Next up, James shows that there are two kinds of wisdom. One is earthly wisdom; the other is heavenly wisdom. One is from above, the other is from below, right here on earth. As we have seen while looking into other books of the Bible, it is important as believers to maintain a heavenly mindset in every situation, even when it is difficult. Having wisdom from above means that you understand the Father's heart and act upon it. It also means that you are focused on prayer and hearing the Lord's perspective on situations. It's all about relationship—not religion. Approaching situations with earthly wisdom is what happens when we rely on our own experience to direct our response. Every one of us has come from a different background that has informed our way of thinking. For example, some of us are street smart while others are book smart.

James shows that the goal is not to make decisions in the same way as our peers do, but to reach for wisdom from above instead. For that is where the ultimate wisdom lies.

Wealth

The last topic James looks at is wealth and the negative impact it can have on us and on the poor. Thanks to social media and the entertainment industry, we are constantly being told what is cool, right, and sexy. Every ad tries to show us what kind of lifestyle we could be living if we just had their product in our lives. Ads try to make us feel as if we are missing out on something if we don't give in and buy the advertised product. But once we buy it, there is always something bigger and better coming along that we will want next. It's a never-ending cycle. Citizens of the United States of America have a lot of money. As a whole, we are very wealthy. And yet we have *a lot* of problems.

The audience James was writing to also had a lot of problems, many of which revolved around money. They were ignoring the poor and were completely self-centered in their pursuits—two things that should not characterize us as believers in Jesus.

James's audience needed to redirect their money mindset and share the love of Christ with everyone around them, rich or poor. One thing I must state is that money itself is never the problem. I know many believers who are absolutely loaded. It's the *love of money* that is at the root of all kinds of evil (see 1 Timothy 6:10). It's a heart issue.

So trials, faith and works, the tongue, wisdom, and wealth—those are the five areas James breaks down throughout this book. ■

DAY 52

Read James 1–5

▶ Can you remember any times of great testing in your life? What about times of tempting?

▶ After you became a believer, did you notice any change in your actions? If so, what specifically happened?

▶ Can you think of a time when you wish you would have either spoken up or kept your mouth shut? If so, what happened?

▶ Out of the five themes we just looked at in the book of James, which one would you like to improve on? Why? What are some things you can do today to begin the improvement process?

gifted saints

1 Peter

AUTHOR

The author of 1 Peter is the apostle Peter. Peter was the leader of the twelve disciples. With that said, Peter was the first pastor who founded the church after Jesus ascended to heaven. Peter was one of Jesus's closest disciples, even though he denied Jesus three times.

DATE

Peter likely wrote this first letter around AD 64 near the beginning of Nero's persecution of Christians. Who was Nero and what was his deal?

Nero was the Roman emperor who reigned from AD 54–68. He was an average emperor at the beginning of his reign, but then things took a turn for the worse around AD 64 during the Great Fire of Rome. The Roman citizens blamed him for starting the fire because they knew he had grand plans for the city. And to cover his tracks, he blamed the fire on the Christians. From then on, the persecution of Christians ramped up in disgusting ways as Nero did anything to gain popularity. He would torture Christians by crucifying them, using them as entertainment in fights against lions, and most horrifically, soaking them in oil and impaling them on a pole in his garden to be used as a source of light for his dinner parties.

Rome was anything but a pretty sight for Christians. Word was getting out among churches all over the Greco-Roman world about what was happening, so Peter wrote to them in preparation for what was to come. He knew he would be crucified eventually, so this was one of his last forms of contact with them.

AUDIENCE

Peter wrote this letter to the Twelve Tribes of the Dispersion that were spread out around Asia Minor. Remember, Paul was the missionary to the Gentiles, while Peter was the missionary to the Jews.

REASON

Peter was writing to encourage the believers to remain holy in their suffering and to submit to authority in hopes of sharing love and peace.

THEME

Suffer now and be taken care of later.

OVERVIEW

First Peter is a book of persecution and warning for what was to come in the near future. As things get crazier in our world every day and Christians are persecuted more and more, this book is very relevant for us. As we saw in the Gospels, Jesus always said that there would be persecution and suffering for those who believed in Him. Jesus is worth more than the cost of any persecution we might suffer, and we can hold on to that promise until we meet Him. Though persecution may come, Peter also teaches that we have been born into a royal priesthood. That means we are princes and princesses. We are *royalty*. But so many times we fail to act like it because we don't want to appear conceited. That's garbage. God is saying that you and I are royalty, children of the King, so we need to believe what He says about us! We are a special group. We are a holy nation. Transforming our minds to accept this truth is crucial in understanding our identity.

Peter brings up the fact that we are the temple of God (see 1 Peter 2:5). We are His dwelling place on earth. He resides inside of us. That means He can now be anywhere that we are. Since God dwells within His children, we should be cautious about how we treat our bodies. Believers should be fit, joyful, peaceful, and walking in His strength and power. Peter makes it clear that suffering is to be expected. It's part of the normal Christian life. But if your foundation is built on Jesus Christ, you will press on and be rewarded greatly later on. Perseverance in our Christian walk is crucial, especially in a time when society is doing everything it can to veer us away from the cross.

Learning how to submit to authority is one way we can persevere. We have a job to pray for our governmental leaders whether we agree with their decisions or not. We should, however, stand up against their decisions when they go against Scripture. It can be tough to pray for people we don't agree with, but it is also one of the most humbling things we can do.

Peter makes it clear throughout this letter that we are to suffer as Christ suffered. Think about the way Christ suffered and remember, no matter what kind of suffering you may experience now, you will be greatly rewarded in heaven for all of eternity. The best is yet to come! ■

DAY 53

Read 1 Peter 1–5

▶ In what ways have you experienced physical, spiritual, or mental persecution?

▶ Why do you think Christians are more likely to deal with persecution?

▶ How can we honor our governmental leaders even when we don't agree with some of their choices?

▶ Pick one person you know who is not a believer. Write out a prayer plan for them and how you want to see God move in their life.

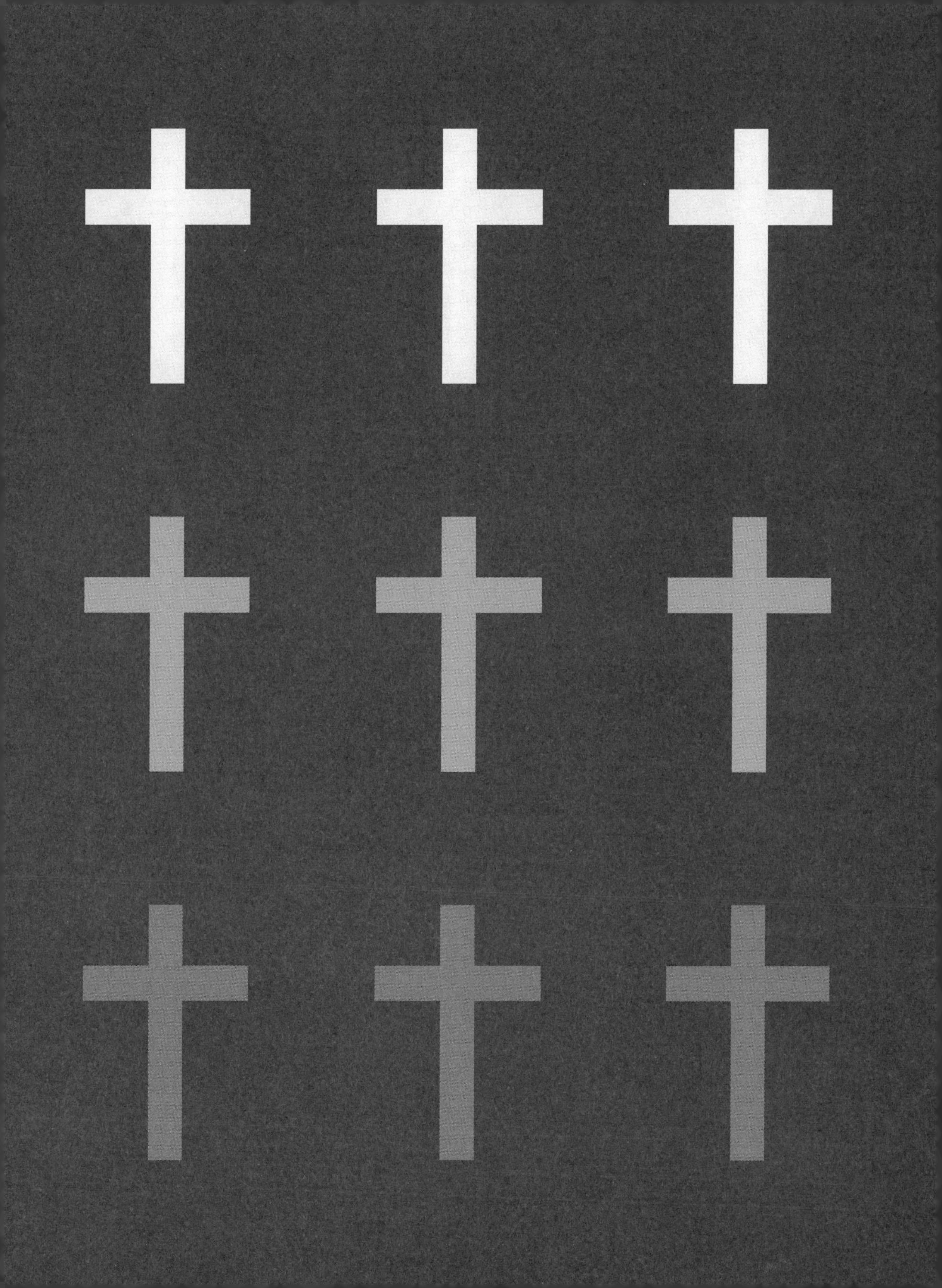

2 Peter

AUTHOR

The second letter of Peter was also written by the apostle Peter.

DATE

Peter knew that his death was right around the corner because of how bad the persecution of Christians had gotten in Rome. He likely penned this last letter around AD 66.

AUDIENCE

Peter is writing to the same group of people that he did in his first letter, the churches in Asia Minor.

REASON

Peter wrote this second letter because false teaching was at an all-time high, and their doctrine was becoming blurred. He is encouraging them to stick to the truth.

THEME

Watch out for false teachers.

KEY VERSES

"Therefore, dear friends, since you have been forewarned, be on your guard so that you may not be carried away by the error of the lawless and fall from your secure position. But grow in the grace and knowledge of our Lord and Savior Jesus Christ. To him be glory both now and forever! Amen." (2 Peter 3:17–18 NIV)

Second Peter has a layout similar to that of 1 Peter, in the sense that it focuses on salvation, warnings, and how to deal with what is ahead. Both letters focus on having a strong foundation so that we will not be shaken.

Through God's promises, Peter writes, we can "become partakers in the divine nature" (1:4). Peter doesn't say that we become God, as Buddhism or New Age beliefs may suggest, but we are going from glory to glory, becoming more like Christ every day, as we read in 2 Corinthians 3:18. When we get to Jude later on, you will realize that 2 Peter 2 is almost word for word the same as Jude. Whereas the mockers are actually present in Jude, 2 Peter shows that they are still in the future, so Peter most likely wrote first. It can be assumed that the two of them were friends though, since Jude was Jesus's brother. The same problems were present in both of their churches. Peter and Jude both knew that if there was false teaching in the church, it wouldn't matter how much persecution they endured because the church would crumble from the inside out. That's why Peter is again emphasizing how important it is to have a strong foundation. If they have a scriptural understanding of salvation, they will be able to discern between what is true and what is of the enemy.

When I studied 2 Peter for the first time, I thought that it was a book I couldn't really relate to. When Peter talked about false teachers that didn't click with me whatsoever because I didn't think that was an issue in the church today—at all. Then I began to study some of the beliefs of various current denominations, and I was shocked to realize that there is false teaching going on EVERYWHERE. I am blown away by how unbiblical some teachings are, yet people believe it because they don't know the Bible for themselves.

Well guess what:

The belief that you must repent through another person is NOT biblical.

The belief that miracles no longer happen is NOT biblical.

The belief that the Holy Spirit is no longer relevant is NOT biblical.

The belief that child baptism covers you for life is NOT biblical.

There are many things taught in some churches today that are just flat-out lies, but you wouldn't know that unless you knew the truth. That's why I am so proud of you for taking the time to dive into the Word this year and learn for yourself what is and what is not of God. We have two of the greatest gifts in the world available 24/7: the Holy Spirit and the Bible. Don't let a day slip away without taking advantage of each of them. Spend some time in prayer this week thanking God for providing you with the desire to study His Word. Also, ask Him to open your eyes to see what is from Him and what is a lie that has masqueraded as truth in your life. ∎

DAY 54

Read 2 Peter 1–3

▶ What can you do today to increase in each of the qualities Peter lists in 2 Peter 1:5–7? Make a list of what you need to improve on.

▶ How can you respond to people who make fun of your beliefs or mock you?

▶ What are some things you can do to have more of an eternal mindset in your day-to-day life?

▶ How should we deal with false teaching?

1, 2, and 3 John

FIRST LETTER

AUTHOR

The apostle John wrote all three letters at the end of his thirty-year residence in Ephesus.

DATE

These three letters were written before his death in AD 98 and after he wrote his Gospel, making it around AD 90–95.

AUDIENCE

John's first letter was written to the churches in Asia Minor, surrounding where he lived in Ephesus. He had an amazing relationship with all the churches after being there for thirty years, and they were all in true fellowship with one another.

REASON

John wrote this first letter to focus even more on fellowship within their communities, to teach them more about sin, to confirm their salvation and to discredit any false teaching that was infiltrating the area.

THEME

Security in eternal life.

KEY VERSE

"I write these things to you who believe in the name of the Son of God, that you may know that you have eternal life" (1 John 5:13).

OVERVIEW

As is apparent in this letter, John sees things in a very black-and-white manner. Everything in life falls into one of two categories: It's either good or evil. You are influenced by both and can choose which one you want to focus on. Just as we saw in the Gospel of John and will see again in Revelation, John writes in sevens. He knows the divine importance of the number and follows that structure throughout his main points.

In this letter, he has seven main contrasts he looks at:

- Light and darkness
- Truth and lies
- Loving the father and loving the world
- Life and death
- Children of God and children of the devil
- Love and hate
- Good works and bad works

What happens to darkness when you flip on a light? It disappears. The same is with Christ. We know that He *is* light and since He is inside of us then we also are light. That is a profound revelation to have. That means whenever we go into a dark area, it is no longer dark because we are there. Christ in us exposes the darkness and makes it disappear. Having that realization should develop confidence for the next time you are in a place that lacks the presence of God. We can overpower any tactic the enemy uses against us based on Jesus's shed blood and who we are in Christ. That's amazing stuff right there.

The life of a Christian is about this process called sanctification, which we explored in Galatians. It's the work the Holy Spirit does in our lives internally. When I decided to start pursuing Christ with all of my heart, He had some serious cleaning up to do. I felt like a punching bag, getting swung left and right in order to change my thoughts and desires personally, professionally, and relationally. I admit that I still struggle with changing, but the intensity of the battle has decreased as I have become more and more like Jesus. That's what John is getting at. The closer you get to Christ, the less sin will have an impact on your day.

Our desire should be to become more Christlike. If you are truly pursuing Him, there should be visible signs of progress being made. As a new creation, walking by the Spirit, it is not natural for us to sin anymore. We do still sin, but it is no longer our nature. The seed of God inside of us contradicts the influence of the devil on the outside of us. Sin is no joke, and God doesn't take it lightly. We must redirect our focus to allow Him to do work inside of us and be used for His greater purpose. John wants us to have confidence in our new nature. We are now living on the opposite side of the spectrum compared with what we used to know. Life really is just as black and white as John makes it. There's good and evil. Pick a side.

SECOND LETTER

AUDIENCE

The audience of 2 John is widely debated because he does not specify who the "elect lady and her children" in the greeting are. That leaves it up to you to decide between the three main options that I have encountered:

First, John could be writing to an unknown woman who has her own house church, most likely in Ephesus.

Second, John could be writing to a church as a whole and its members. The "elect lady" would be the church itself, her "children" could be the members, and her "sister" could be another church.

Third, which is rarely taught but makes the most sense to me, is that John was writing to Mary, the mother of Jesus. Mary would have been known as an "elect lady," considering she was the mother of Jesus

Christ. We know that she had other children and a sister. Also, John was told by Jesus to look after her, which would go in line with the topic of this letter.

But we don't know for sure, and quite frankly, it isn't that important.

REASON

John writes as a warning against showing hospitality to false teachers.

THEME

Hospitality.

KEY VERSE

"If anyone comes to you and does not bring this teaching, do not receive him into your house or give him any greeting" (2 John 10).

THIRD LETTER

AUDIENCE

John wrote his third letter to a man named Gaius who had a house church somewhere in Asia Minor.

REASON

John wrote to encourage Gaius in his love for hospitality, to deal with the pride of Diotrephes, and to tell them to accept the teaching of Demetrius.

THEME

Be accepting of other believers.

OVERVIEW

These two letters by John are short, nearly identical letters that are written to a man and a woman. Both needed to be written from a different angle in order to adapt the different ways men and women think. The main issue for both was the topic of hospitality. John writes to the elect lady as a warning against showing hospitality to false teachers. That's about it for this letter.

John wrote his third letter to a man named Gaius to encourage him in his love for hospitality, to deal with the pride of Diotrephes, and to tell the house church to accept the teaching of Demetrius. Third John is basically instructing the church to be accepting of other believers.

As I mentioned, John is telling the recipients of his second and third letters how to be better at showing hospitality. The woman needed to be more cautious, and the man needed to be more open. There were many missionaries going around in the Greco-Roman world, and they were dependent on the hospitality of other believers. That situation allowed for false teaching to spread because anybody who was a "believer" was accepted. ◼

one body

one mind

one church

one God

▶ What does it mean to be a citizen of heaven while here on earth?

▶ What do you think "God is love" (1 John 4:8) means?

▶ Who is the most hospitable person you know? What makes them special?

▶ How can you be more hospitable to other believers?

Jude

AUTHOR

The author of Jude is "Jude, a servant of Jesus Christ and brother of James" (1:1). That would make both Jude and James half-brothers of Jesus.

DATE

Jude was written shortly before or after 2 Peter, but before the destruction of the temple in AD 70, likely making it between AD 67 and 69.

AUDIENCE

Jude most likely wrote to believers from the Dispersion who were possibly located in Antioch since it was a hub and easily accessible for false teachers.

REASON

Jude wrote because false teachers were influencing the church and causing believers to stray. Jude is encouraging them to stay strong and fight for their faith.

THEME

Contend for the faith.

KEY VERSE

"Beloved, although I was very eager to write to you about our common salvation, I found it necessary to write appealing to you to contend for the faith that was once for all delivered to the saints" (Jude 3).

Jude is a book many people skip over because they don't understand the importance of it. And honestly, it is a pretty strange one. If you compare it to 2 Peter 2, it's almost the same letter too. Jude addresses a few problems the audience is facing, which began with a group of false teachers who were teaching that you could abuse grace. They were saying that once you were saved, you could sin all you wanted to and it didn't matter. That's not the Father's heart at all.

Yes, grace covers us when we mess up, but our lifestyle should no longer reflect a life of sin. We are new creations and have the power inside of us to live righteously, to go from glory to glory.

Secondly, the false teachers were teaching that Jesus was not the ONLY way to heaven, but just ONE of the ways. I don't need to explain that one. You know Jesus is the only way.

The focus needs to be on following Scripture and modeling the Father's heart toward those who have been deceived. That means approaching the situation in a loving, yet firm manner. We need to make the truth known, but our actions must flow from a heart of love. Jude begins characterizing the false teachers as "ungodly" (v. 4). He also uses that word three times in verse 15 to describe them. Their godlessness was a mockery of godliness. Talk about a fitting topic! The church today is constantly being mocked by our culture for its godliness. We have become the brunt of society's jokes. God tells us in His Word that this would happen though, so we can't be too surprised or get too upset when it does.

One thing Jude makes clear is that we are to contend for the gospel. We must fight and stand up for the truth. Jesus is "the way, and the truth, and the life. No one comes to the Father except through" Him (John 14:6). No matter what your peers say, if you remain focused on your relationship with Jesus, then you will always be taken care of. Jude teaches us that we must learn how to contend for the faith.

As things get crazier and crazier in the world, we need to be prepared to stand up for the truth no matter what comes at us. One way to contend for the faith is by memorizing Scripture, holding on to those truths, and sharing them with others. I would encourage you to begin memorizing Scripture if you don't already. Knowing what God says about himself and about you will serve as great reminders when things begin to heat up. ■

Revelation

AUTHOR

The author of Revelation is the apostle John, who also wrote the Gospel of John and three epistles.

DATE

Revelation was written toward the end of John's life and after his other writings, putting it sometime in the mid-90s AD.

AUDIENCE

According to Revelation 1:11, John is writing this book "to the seven churches, to Ephesus and to Smyrna and to Pergamum and to Thyatira and to Sardis and to Philadelphia and to Laodicea."

REASON

John wrote the book of Revelation to show the completion of God's plan.

THEME

The current church and its future.

KEY VERSE

"Write therefore the things that you have seen, those that are and those that are to take place after this" (Revelation 1:19).

OVERVIEW

Revelation has a strange stigma attached to it that causes many people to steer clear of ever attempting to read it. Yet it is the only book in the Bible that promises a blessing upon the reader, which is super interesting to me.

Yes, some of the visions may seem weird to us because they aren't the type of thing we see every day in the natural realm. That's because Revelation is what we call *apocalyptic* writing. It looks into the future from the spiritual realm instead of through the natural perspective. It's the future as God sees it.

Revelation completes the story of redemption. We can hold on to the hope for a better tomorrow based on what God's Word says about the future. This is His promise of what will one day be our reality.

As you begin to study, you should know that there are four main views of how to interpret Revelation:

The *Preterist View* holds that everything in the text happened before AD 70, but there are many critiques that prove this to be impossible.

The *Historicist View* believes that the history of the church is split into seven sections, each being represented by one of the churches listed in Revelation 1:11.

The *Futurist View* has been one of the most popular views in the Western church over the last one hundred years. This view holds that nearly everything in Revelation is meant to be taken literally and viewed as a chronology of events to come, including the Rapture, seven years of tribulation, a thousand-year earthly reign of Jesus, and a major focus on current events.

The *Idealist View* believes the book is meant to be interpreted symbolically in light of Scripture, with a focus on the church being the fulfillment of Israel. The seals, trumpets, and bowls judgments in Revelation represent events taking place ever since the beginning of the Church Age.

I would highly encourage you to research all of these views more in depth, instead of just thinking about the *Left Behind* series and what your church may teach on the subject. My views on all of it have changed over time, and the truth of the matter is that some things in Scripture we won't know until they actually happen. So there are great arguments on all sides, and it's okay to disagree with other people's views. At the end of the day, one view may be right and another view wrong, but it shouldn't influence our salvation; we should all be sharing our testimonies and preaching the gospel no matter what happens. So definitely research the views more deeply online, look at what the early church believed, look at different commentaries, and have fun with it.

Many would state that God's judgment in Revelation is torture for those who didn't follow Him. That is blatantly a false assumption. God's judgment is an act of love. It's a second chance. Amidst judgment, God's granting more time for repentance. For people to fall on their knees before Christ and receive Him as Savior and Lord. God's wrath shows His true heart.

God doesn't want us to spend eternity in hell. He eagerly desires for every single person to spend eternity in the new heaven and the new earth. This was His plan all along—it was never for people to suffer eternally. But God loves us and gives us a choice: We can choose Him or not. He didn't create us to be robots. But rather He desires a relationship with us. He loves us that much—just look at the cross. ■

DAY 56

▶ Jude discusses false teachers. How would you deal with false teachers in your church today?

▶ Do you believe Revelation is meant to be studied literally or symbolically?

▶ In chapter 1 alone there are twenty-four titles or descriptions of Jesus Christ. In all of Scripture there are actually two hundred-some. What titles of Jesus can you think of?

▶ How do you handle criticism? Can you relate to any of the seven churches? If so, what does John suggest you do regarding that trait?

WEEKLY CHECK-IN & PRAYER

▶ What is the most important thing you learned this past week?

▶ How can you apply the teaching to your life?

▶ Write a short prayer for the week ahead.

DAY 57

▶ John describes how everyone is worshiping, praising the King of Kings in heaven. How does worship currently influence your life?

▶ Why do you think God used bowls, seals, and trumpets to describe what was happening?

▶ Who do you think the one hundred forty-four thousand people are in Revelation 7?

▶ How do you reconcile God's wrath during the end times with His being a God of love?

▶ Who do you think the "two witnesses" are from Revelation 11?

▶ Try to describe what the woman, male child, and dragon represent in Revelation 12.

▶ What do you think the mark of the beast is or will be? Why do you think it is placed on your right arm or forehead?

▶ Do you think we are in the beginning stages of the end times?

DAY 59

▶ Do you think Armageddon will be an actual war in the Middle East?

▶ Why do you think God chose Babylon to represent the world?

▶ Why do you think Jesus is represented as a lamb?

▶ If you remember from studying the Gospel of John, he often wrote in sevens (seven miracles, seven "I Am" statements, etc.). What does the number seven represent in Christianity? How many times does Jesus appear in this book?

▶ What do you think the Marriage Supper of the Lamb will be like?

▶ What are your thoughts on hell?

▶ What do you think the new earth will be like? What will we eat? What will we do?

▶ How did you feel about Revelation before reading it vs. after reading it? Why do you think so many people choose not to study it?

FAITH SAYS

HOLD ON

WHEN DOUBT SAYS

LET GO

Congratulations!

You made it. You just accomplished something that many people have never done—studied the entire New Testament, front to back. But *you* did. I am so proud of you, and I know that God is too.

Before we say our goodbyes, there is one final thing I would like you to do. Use the rest of this page to explain the gospel message in an easy-to-understand way that you can use in the future for evangelism.

Matthew 28:19 says, "Go therefore and make disciples of all nations, baptizing them in the name of the Father and of the Son and of the Holy Spirit." Now that you know the Word better, go and share it! Make disciples! Spread the LOVE of our Father!

May God bless you all.
—Z

THE BIBLE IS GOOD FOR YOU

60-DAY REFLECTION

Take a moment to reflect on the past sixty days and how God transformed your heart through the process.

▶ Where are you on your faith journey now?

▶ What was the most important thing God taught you through this process?

▶ How do you plan on continuing to study the Bible?

SAVE

How to Share the Gospel

Sharing your faith with others can be awkward. We get that.

So we broke it down into three easy steps to help you start sharing the gospel today.

Step 1: Understand the gospel. Why is it called "good news"? And why should it be shared?

Step 2: Listen before you speak. What does your friend currently believe?

Step 3: Live it out. Does your life reflect the message you want to share?

Step 1: Understand the gospel. Why is it called Good News? And why should it be shared?

When we read the word *gospel* in the New Testament, it means good news. If you didn't know, the New Testament was originally written in Greek. So this word *gospel* is in Greek *euangelion*. It's where we get the words *evangelist* and *evangelical* from. But our focus today is the Good News.

So why is the gospel Good News?

Well, you have to start by looking at the bad news.

Early on in the first part of the Bible called the Old Testament, we learn about a man named Moses. Now in Moses's day, the nation of Israel, God's chosen people, were in slavery in Egypt. God ends up using Moses to set the people free from slavery through a bunch of different miracles, which is basically God doing something extravagant that doesn't make sense to our minds in the physical realm.

Once the people were free, God gave them what we know as the Law. Yes, the Law was a bunch of rules to follow, but that's because of our sin nature at the time, and God wanted us to live to higher standards. So it was more of a manual on how to live a holy life. The Law stated that the only way to be fully cleansed from sin was through the sacrifice of an innocent life. To us that sounds crazy, but at the time, that was part of the culture.

Eventually the nation of Israel fell away and lost sight of the Law.

Then we get into the second part of the Bible called the New Testament, and a man named Jesus enters the scene. He was announcing that the kingdom of God is here and that God's reign over Israel was being restored.

And it was going to be through Him. This was the Good News.

But the political people at the time didn't like Jesus's message because it threatened their status. Jesus was saying that God's kingdom was going to take over.

So they killed Him.

Little did they know that this sacrifice of an innocent, sinless life is exactly what needed to happen to cover the sins of anyone who believed in Jesus and the message He preached.

But He didn't remain dead. Three days later He rose from the dead, proving that He was the true King and that God's kingdom reigned supreme.

And the best news of all is that Jesus offers to share this victory with us. We are no longer held down by the Law, but we can be free and we can live for eternity in heaven and eventually a new earth. We can't earn our salvation; it's a free gift. That's the best news ever. That's the gospel. And you get to choose whether or not you want to believe it and accept it. One thing I do know is that it's God's heart for you to choose life.

If you want to learn more about the gospel, the first four books of the New Testament are actually called *the Gospels*. They're from different perspectives of guys named Matthew, Mark, Luke, and John. Then you can read the book of Acts to learn how other people began to spread this Good News.

And now it's our responsibility to continue spreading it.

Step 2: Listen before you speak. What does your friend currently believe?

Sharing your faith cannot be done without understanding where the other person currently sits. What are their views on God? Life? Religion? Have they had any good or bad experiences with other Christians?

Too often, Christians attempt to share their faith through passionately talking *at* people, but not *with* them. Sharing your faith begins with a healthy dialogue, and that dialogue happens when you listen.

But listening can be hard. It requires patience, empathy, discernment, and wisdom. When listening is done well, it results in the other person being heard. This is so important. Their responses should help equip you with what to say and what not to say. Don't force anything; keep it natural. It's okay if they don't believe right away—it could take years. Just stay patient and keep the conversation going.

Listening is the key that unlocks communication.

Step 3: Live it out. Does your life reflect the message you want to share?

The most effective way you can share the Gospel is by living it out. Let the Good News of your life be your witness. People notice when you live with a greater sense of hope, peace, joy, and patience. And we know that all of that comes from our relationship with Jesus.

People love to see things in action, and sharing the gospel is no different. When your life aligns with your message, that's when people begin to listen.

And living out the gospel is simple. Follow the lead of Jesus and let love be your guide.

Remember that it's a marathon, not a sprint. Some people will take a long time just to understand why you believe what you believe, and others may never understand. And then there are some who will want exactly what you have. Your sole responsibility in following Jesus is to keep going and let God do the rest. You've got this, and the best is yet to come!

SALVATION PRAYER

If you have a friend who wants to accept Jesus as their Lord and Savior, the next step on their faith journey is to begin a personal relationship with Him, through which they will be saved from the consequences of their sins—death. This is called salvation.

As Christians, we are saved by grace through faith in Jesus Christ. Jesus died and rose again to pay the price for our sins. Salvation doesn't come from our good deeds or by doing anything special; it's a free gift from God just because He loves us so much. We need to turn away from our sins, believe that Jesus Christ is God's Son and our Savior, and submit to Him as Lord of our lives. By doing so, we receive salvation and eternal life. How awesome is that!

If this is something they want for their life, walk them through this prayer:

Jesus, I believe that you are the Son of God and Savior of the world. I believe that you died for my sins and rose from the dead. I believe that through your sacrifice, I am a new person. Forgive me for my sin and fill me with your Spirit. Today, I choose to follow you for the rest of my life as Lord of my life. Amen.

YOUR FRIEND'S NEXT STEPS

- Find a local church community to get plugged into.
- Try to read the Bible and spend time in prayer for at least ten to fifteen minutes every day.
- Get baptized.

Trivia Questions and Answers

1. What does the word *gospel* mean?
2. Which books make up the four Gospels?
3. Who was Matthew writing to in the Gospel of Matthew?
4. Who were the parents of Jesus?
5. What town was Jesus born in?
6. When Jesus was a baby, who wanted to kill Him?
7. Who was the mother of John the Baptist?
8. Where was Jesus found when His parents lost Him?
9. What did John the Baptist say when he saw Jesus?
10. During Jesus's baptism, what form did the Holy Spirit take?
11. At what age did Jesus start His ministry?
12. How long was Jesus in the wilderness where He was tempted by Satan?
13. What was the first temptation of Jesus?
14. What was the purpose of Jesus coming to earth?
15. What does the word *Gentile* mean?
16. What does the word *Rabbi* mean?
17. What is a disciple?
18. What words does Jesus use when recruiting His disciples?
19. What was Jesus's first miracle?
20. Which disciple called himself the one "whom Jesus loved"?
21. What nationality was the woman at the well?
22. Which disciple tried to walk on water with Jesus?
23. Which disciple was a tax collector before following Jesus?
24. What was the name of the man who asked Jesus to heal his daughter, who was dying?
25. What type of servant is Jesus referred to in Mark?
26. What did Jesus use to feed the five thousand?
27. After Jesus healed the blind man in Bethsaida, what did Jesus tell him not to do?
28. If you want to follow Jesus, you must pick up your what?
29. What type of tree did Jesus curse?

30. Jesus said that "it is easier for a camel to go through the eye of a needle" than for a rich person to do what?

31. Why shouldn't we give anyone on earth the title *father*?

32. Which two prophets showed up at the Mount of Transfiguration with Jesus?

33. How many pieces of silver did Judas receive for betraying Jesus?

34. The Gospel of John focuses on Jesus being fully God and fully what?

35. What three parts make up the Trinity?

36. Which Gospel talks about the Holy Spirit most?

37. What is the shortest verse in the Bible?

38. After Lazarus died, what did Jesus say at the entrance of his tomb?

39. How many "I am" statements are in the Gospel of John?

40. What are all of Jesus's "I am" statements in the Gospel of John?

41. How are we able to get to know God the Father?

42. What animal does Jesus ride into Jerusalem on?

43. In communion, what do the bread and wine represent?

44. How long was Jesus in the tomb?

45. How long was Jesus on earth between His resurrection and ascension?

46. After Jesus was resurrected, how many times did He ask Peter if he loved Him?

47. Which three languages were written on the notice that Pilate placed on Jesus's cross?

48. What was the significance of the temple veil being torn in two?

49. How is Jesus represented in regard to Passover?

50. What does it mean to repent?

51. What was Luke's occupation?

52. What disciple replaced Judas Iscariot after he betrayed Jesus?

53. What happens to the disciples and other believers at the beginning of Acts?

54. How many people are added to the church on the day of Pentecost in Acts?

55. Who is stoned to death for their faith in Jesus?

56. Who watched the coats of the men stoning Stephen?

57. What was Paul's Jewish name?

58. Who was Paul's rabbi?

59. What city was Paul heading to when he met Jesus?

60. What was the name of Paul's hometown?

61. Who did Paul study under before his conversion?

62. Who joined Paul on his first missionary journey?

63. What was the Jerusalem Council?

64. How many missionary journeys did Paul go on?

65. What island was Paul shipwrecked on?

66. Who was in prison with Paul when their chains were loosened after singing worship music?

67. What is an epistle?

68. Who wrote the majority of the New Testament letters?

69. What does Paul say can separate us from the love of God?

70. What does sanctification mean?

71. What chapter in the New Testament is considered the "love chapter"?

72. Which spiritual gift does Paul say we should especially "earnestly desire"?

73. Where the spirit of the Lord is, there is what?

74. How many characteristics are the fruit of the Holy Spirit?

75. What characteristics make up the fruit of the Holy Spirit?

76. Who was the book of Ephesians written to?

77. In the "armor of God" from Ephesians 6, what does the sword represent?

78. Which part of the armor of God is associated with salvation?

79. How does the book of Ephesians say that children can live a long life on earth?

80. From where did Paul write the book of Philippians?

81. Which letters from Paul are known as the *prison epistles*?

82. How often are believers instructed to pray?

83. Which letters from Paul are known as the *pastoral epistles*?

84. What role does Paul play in the life of Timothy?

85. Aside from Paul, what other man influenced Timothy's faith?

86. What is the only letter of recommendation in the Bible?

87. In the book of Philemon, who is Paul asking forgiveness for?

88. The Word of God is sharper than what?

89. What chapter of the Bible is considered the "Hall of Faith"?

90. What five books did John write?

91. According to the book of James, faith without what is dead?

92. What is the purpose of spiritual gifts?

93. What was the last book Paul wrote before his death?

94. How long will the kingdom of God last?

95. In the book of Jude, which archangel is said to have argued with the devil over the body of Moses?

96. What is the shortest book of the New Testament?

97. What island did John have the vision of Revelation on?

98. What is the only book of the Bible that says you will be blessed by reading it?

99. What number does John repeat throughout the book of Revelation?

100. According to Revelation, how long will Jesus reign on earth after His second coming?

TRIVIA ANSWERS

1. Good news
2. Matthew, Mark, Luke, and John
3. The Jews
4. Mary and Joseph (Luke 2:1–8)
5. Bethlehem (Matthew 2:1)
6. Herod the Great (Matthew 2:13)
7. Elizabeth (Luke 1:13)
8. The temple (Luke 2:41–52)
9. "Behold, the Lamb of God" (John 1:29)
10. A dove (Luke 3:22)
11. About thirty (Luke 3:23)
12. Forty days (Matthew 4:2)
13. To turn stones into bread (Matthew 4:3)
14. To seek and save the lost (Luke 19:10)
15. A person who is non-Jewish
16. Teacher
17. A student or apprentice
18. "Follow me" (Matthew 9:9; Mark 1:17; Luke 5:27; John 1:43)
19. Turning water into wine (John 2:9)
20. John (John 13:23)
21. Samaritan (John 4:7)
22. Peter (Matthew 14:29)
23. Matthew (Matthew 9:9)
24. Jairus (Mark 5:22)
25. Suffering servant (Mark 8:31)
26. Five loaves and two fish (Mark 6:38)
27. Do not go into the city (Mark 8:26)
28. Cross (Mark 8:34)
29. A fig tree (Mark 11:13–14)
30. Enter the kingdom of God (Mark 10:25)
31. We have one Father who is in heaven (Matthew 23:9)
32. Elijah and Moses (Matthew 17:3)
33. Thirty (Matthew 26:15)
34. Human/man
35. God the Father, God the Son, and God the Holy Spirit
36. Luke
37. "Jesus wept." (John 11:35)
38. "Lazarus, come out." (John 11:43)

39. Seven (John 6:35; 8:12; 10:9; 10:11; 11:25; 14:6; 15:5)
40. "I am the bread of life" (John 6:35); "I am the light of the world" (John 8:12); "I am the door" of the sheep (John 10:7–9); "I am the resurrection and the life" (John 11:25); "I am the good shepherd" (John 10:11); "I am the way, and the truth, and the life" (John 14:6); "I am the true vine" (John 15:1).
41. Only through Jesus (John 14:6)
42. A donkey (John 12:14)
43. Jesus's broken body and His blood (Luke 22:19–20)
44. Three days and three nights (Matthew 12:40)
45. Forty days (Acts 1:3)
46. Three (John 21:15–17)
47. Aramaic, Latin, and Greek (John 19:20)
48. A relationship with God was now available to all people through Jesus's atoning sacrifice.
49. As the Lamb of God (John 1:29)
50. To acknowledge and turn away from your sins
51. Physician (Colossians 4:14)
52. Matthias (Acts 1:26)
53. They are filled with the Holy Spirit (Acts 2:4)
54. Three thousand (Acts 2:41)
55. Stephen (Acts 7:59–60)
56. Paul (Acts 7:58)
57. Saul (Acts 13:9)
58. Gamaliel (Acts 22:3)
59. Damascus (Acts 9:3)
60. Tarsus (Acts 21:39)
61. Gamaliel (Acts 22:3)
62. Barnabas (Acts 13:2–3)
63. A meeting to decide if Gentile Christians needed to observe Mosaic Law (Acts 15)
64. Four (Acts 13:4–15:35; 15:36–18:22; 18:23–21:17)
65. Malta (Acts 28:1)

66. Silas (Acts 16:25–26)
67. A letter
68. Paul
69. Nothing (Romans 8:38–39)
70. The process of becoming holy
71. 1 Corinthians 13
72. Prophecy (1 Corinthians 14:1)
73. Liberty (2 Corinthians 3:17)
74. Nine (Galatians 5:22–23)
75. Love, joy, peace, patience, kindness, goodness, faithfulness, gentleness, self-control (Galatians 5:22–23)
76. The church in Ephesus (Ephesians 1:1)
77. The sword of the Spirit, aka the Bible (Ephesians 6:17)
78. The helmet (Ephesians 6:17)
79. By honoring their parents (Ephesians 6:2–3)
80. Jail (Philippians 1:13)
81. Ephesians, Philippians, Colossians, and Philemon
82. Continually (1 Thessalonians 5:17)
83. 1 and 2 Timothy and Titus
84. His spiritual father (1 Timothy 1:2)
85. Barnabas
86. The book of Philemon
87. Onesimus (Philemon 1:10)
88. Any double-edged sword (Hebrews 4:12)
89. Hebrews 11
90. Gospel of John, 1 John, 2 John, 3 John, and Revelation
91. Works (James 2:17)
92. To serve one another and to bring glory to Jesus (1 Peter 4:10–11)
93. Second Timothy
94. Forever (2 Peter 1:11)
95. Michael (Jude 1:9)
96. Jude
97. The Island of Patmos (Revelation 1:9–11)
98. Revelation (Revelation 1:3)
99. Seven (Revelation 1:4, 5:6, 10:3, etc.)
100. A thousand years (Revelation 20:4)

Acknowledgments

In 2014 I moved to Australia with a Bible and a handful of pressing questions: Is God real? Is the Bible true? Do I want to continue pursuing the faith of my childhood?

I was questioning it all. And I wanted to be true to myself. If I were to consider myself a Christian, I should at least know the Bible, right? So I went through a program where we studied Scripture as intensely as I possibly could: twelve hours a day, six days a week. The trajectory of my life was forever changed.

This book is a culmination of my time in Australia mixed with what I have learned in my personal studies. The people who have positively influenced my relationship with God are countless, but a few people I am deeply grateful for are:

Gisela, my love, for your patience, kindness, and brilliance. These books are just as much you as they are me. I love you.

Pete and T, mom and dad, for always praying for me to have a passion for God's Word even when I was my furthest from Him. It worked.

Tony and Elsa, my "in-loves," for teaching me how to bring God into every moment and inspiring me to go even deeper in Scripture.

Bryan Hunsberger for creating a safe space for people to wrestle with Scripture and fall in love with Jesus. I cherish every moment on the Sunshine Coast. You sparked all of this within me.

The Brand Sunday team for working tirelessly on every new project to bring people closer to God and make the Bible less overwhelming. You all inspire me endlessly.

Jeff Braun and the entire Bethany House team for taking a chance on me and bringing this to more people than I could have ever imagined.

Sharon Hodge, my editor extraordinaire, for catching all my mistakes and encouraging me to keep writing.

JESUS + NOTHING
JESUS + NOTHING
JESUS + NOTHING
JESUS + NOTHING
JESUS + NOTHING

ZACH WINDAHL is an entrepreneur, author, and coach with a passion for creating resources and products that help others see the good in their everyday lives and grow in their faith. He is the founder of The Brand Sunday, a company that creates resources to help people understand the Bible, and he hosts guided tours of the Holy Land in Israel each year, helping bring the Bible to life. Marrying his passion for entrepreneurship and making faith simple and attainable has landed Zach in a unique place in the Christian landscape, where he reaches hundreds of thousands of followers on social media and thinks outside the cynical box that is so common in people today. Zach lives in Orlando with his wife, Gisela, and their mini bernedoodle, Nyla. Learn more at ZachWindahl.com.